DIRECT AF SALES

A Daily System for Entrepreneurs Who Want to Dominate Within the Network Marketing Profession

BY

Lisa Hocker

Ordering Information: Quantity sales. Special discounts are available on quantity purchases by corporations, associations, and others. Orders by U.S. trade bookstores and wholesalers.

www.DreamStartersPublishing.com

Table of Contents

Acknowledgements 4

Direct AF Core Values 5

Introduction 13

From a Prosecutor to an Entrepreneur 25

You Actually Can't Start with Your Why 36

Method and Mindset 55

Step One: Create Your Master List 71

Step Two: Reach Out + Invite People to Learn More 78

Step Three: The Fortune is in the Follow Up 91

Step Four: 30 or More Samples Out a Month 102

Step Five: Social Media 105

Accepting Reality 109

Direct Sales is a Journey of Personal Development 116

Why YOU Will Succeed When Most Will Not 124

Conclusion 132

References 137

Accelerate Your Business Results 138

Testimonials 139

Acknowledgements

A special note of gratitude to:

My family, for supporting, listening, encouraging and tolerating me throughout this journey.

Tamra Leigh Wilson, for… everything. We both know none of this would not have happened but for our *years* of conversation, prayer, and your encouragement.

Bridget Cavanaugh, for saying exactly the right words at the right moments enabling me to pick this project up again and finish it. If not for our collaboration, the sales dice would not have come to be.

Team Believe

My Arete family

Direct AF Core Values

1. Always do the right thing – integrity

2. Be Humble – humility and compassion

3. Commit To Excellence – ambition

4. Maintain Relentless Discipline

5. Be A Lifetime Student – learning + personal development

6. Be of Service - gratitude +thankfulness

It is essential that you know your Core Values. Your core values are the values that you hold above all else in your life and in your business. Knowing your core values and what you stand for, what your non-negotiales are, will help you grow from where you are today to where you want to be.

Identify your core values and apply them as you learn and implement the Five Daily Steps. Use this chart to contemplate and identify your specific core values.

Acceptance	Accomplishment	Accountability
Accuracy	Achievement	Adaptability
Agility	Alertness	Altruism
Ambition	Amusement	Assertiveness
Attentive	Awareness	Balance
Beauty	Boldness	Bravery
Brilliance	Calm	Candor
Capable	Careful	Certainty
Challenge	Charity	Cleanliness
Clarity	Clever	Comfort
Commitment	Common sense	Communication
Community	Compassion	Competence
Concentration	Confidence	Connection

Consciousness	Consistency	Contentment
Contribution	Control	Conviction
Cooperation	Courage	Courtesy
Creation	Creativity	Credibility
Curiosity	Decisive	Decisiveness
Dedication	Dependability	Determination
Development	Devotion	Dignity
Discipline	Discovery	Drive
Effectiveness	Efficiency	Empathy
Empower	Endurance	Energy
Enjoyment	Enthusiasm	Equality
Ethical	Excellence	Experience
Exploration	Expressive	Fairness

Family	Famous	Fearless
Feelings	Ferocious	Fidelity
Focus	Foresight	Fortitude
Freedom	Friendship	Fun
Generosity	Genius	Giving
Goodness	Grace	Gratitude
Greatness	Growth	Happiness
Hard work	Harmony	Health
Honesty	Honor	Hope
Humility	Imagination	Improvement
Independence	Individuality	Innovation
Inquisitive	Insightful	Inspiring
Integrity	Intelligence	Intensity

Intuitive	Irreverent	Joy
Justice	Kindness	Knowledge
Lawful	Leadership	Learning
Liberty	Logic	Love
Loyalty	Mastery	Maturity
Meaning	Moderation	Motivation
Openness	Optimism	Order
Organization	Originality	Passion
Patience	Peace	Performance
Persistence	Playfulness	Poise
Potential	Power	Positive
Present	Productivity	Professionalism
Prosperity	Purpose	Quality

Realistic	Reason	Recognition
Recreation	Reflective	Respect
Responsibility	Restraint	Results-oriented
Reverence	Rigor	Risk
Satisfaction	Security	Self-reliance
Self-Expression	Selfless	Sensitivity
Serenity	Service	Sharing
Significance	Silence	Simplicity
Sincerity	Skill	Skillfulness
Smart	Solitude	Spirit
Spirituality	Spontaneous	Stability
Status	Stewardship	Strength

Structure	Success	Support
Surprise	Sustainability	Talent
Teamwork	Temperance	Thankful
Thorough	Thoughtful	Timeliness
Tolerance	Toughness	Traditional
Tranquility	Transparency	Trust
Trustworthy	Truth	Understanding
Uniqueness	Unity	Valor
Victory	Vigor	Vision
Vitality	Wealth	Welcoming
Winning	Wisdom	Wonder

"Entrepreneurs aren't geniuses. Entrepreneurs are people that don't quit".

Andy Frisella

Introduction

"Our deepest fear is not that we are inadequate. Our deepest fear is that we are powerful beyond measure. It is our light, not our darkness that most frightens us. We ask ourselves, 'Who am I to be brilliant, gorgeous, talented, fabulous?' Actually, who are you not to be? You are a child of God. Your playing small does not serve the world. There is nothing enlightened about shrinking so that other people won't feel insecure around you. We are all meant to shine, as children do. We were born to make manifest the glory of God that is within us. It is not just in some of us; it's in everyone. And as we let our light shine, we unconsciously permit other people to do the same. As we are liberated from our fear, our presence automatically liberates others." - Marianne Williamson, A Return to Love: Reflections on the Principles of "A Course in Miracles".

Isn't that just an absolutely beautiful piece of writing? It speaks so deeply to me. During the course of thinking about writing this book, and then actually writing it, I came back to it over and over again because it gave me the courage and strength to start, write, edit and actually finish this book. So many of us stay stuck in our lives, not taking risks, keeping quiet and comfortable because of our own fears and limiting beliefs that were either developed when we were young, or self-imposed along the road we've been down. What if we were able to start a new road, carve out a new path for ourselves where we were able to go through the process of actually moving through all the muck, and fear, and scarcity mindset? What if we actually decided it was time for us and we just chose to walk in the steps toward out own greatness and accomplishments, being able to shrug off those heavy feelings of fear and of being not enough?

Are you afraid of failing, or succeeding? Both will keep you in your stuck in a box, unable to move into your best version of yourself. Are you fearful of the unknown? Or just of fear itself? Whatever your particular fear or fears happen to be, I'm stating and declaring here and now that you can move *through* it and be as big of a success as you decide you will be. In fact, I'll be so bold as to state and declare here and now that by the time you finish this book, you will be able to step into immediate action *even inside of whatever fear you are holding* and as you continue taking action with the Five Daily Steps, your belief and confidence will bloom and your fears will get smaller and hold less significance. You have to decide. Just make a decision. Will you choose to move into action or will you read the book and kind of just move onto the next thing? Will you look around for something easier?

You have to understand that any fears, limiting beliefs or scarcity mindset that you have has been something you've held onto for quite some time. If you may be feeling that you are in a bit of a quandary, don't worry. You've started or you're about to start a new business, or you've been in network marketing for some time and you want to build bigger, or earn more money, or achieve some title or goal. But your fears, limiting beliefs and/or scarcity mindset is holding you back or keeping you stuck. What's a network marketer to do?

The answer is inside this book, inside the simplicity of the system I call the Five Daily Steps that you will learn here. You see, you have got to understand this one basic principle:

Action must be taken before belief is formed and confidence is grown.

Action comes before belief. Once you understand this, you will be able to achieve your goals. Let me give you an example. Have you ever seen a baby who is crawling and is just about ready to learn how to walk? In my lifetime, I have never heard of or seen a situation where a grown-up has to motivate, encourage, inspire or incentivize a crawling baby to learn how to walk. It's a process that happens naturally, right? The baby starts by pulling himself or herself up on a coffee table or on someone's pant leg or on the side of a couch. The baby pulls up and falls down, pulls up and falls down, over and over again until the baby's muscles begin to strengthen. It is in the process of trying and failing, over and over again, that success is born. Eventually, the baby decides

15

he or she is ready to take the next step and move away from the couch or the coffee table and begins to wobbly take his or her first few steps!

Here's my point: do you think that baby needed **belief** before he or she started the process of learning how to walk, or crawl for that matter? Do you think the baby needed to rid herself of any fears or limiting beliefs she held about herself and her ability to succeed at walking? NO! Of course not! In fact, the idea is silly, isn't it?

The baby simply took action! After a few times of being able to pull himself up and hold onto a coffee table, the baby began to get stronger and recognized internally that he could do it! He was capable! And then, when his little leg muscles and confidence got strong enough, he turned away from the couch and took a few steps on his very own! And the pattern continues.

Same with direct selling! You MUST take a small action, see a result, grow your belief, increase your confidence which then leads to you to take more small actions, see even more results and increase confidence even more! Notice that fear doesn't have room in this equation.

Action --- > Belief --- > Confidence

Besides teaching you the Five Daily Steps, this book will teach you and help you to fully understand that you are capable and will have to take that first small action while you are currently living with and experiencing whatever fears, limiting beliefs and/or scarcity mindset that you are choosing to carry around. This book may help you in terms of you coming to a place where you are able to let these go, but I'll tell you now, my friend, you are going to have to implement the actions even while holding the fear.

You ready? Let's get into it. The direct selling and network marketing profession has been around for years and has endured the test of time. The problem for some people is that they simply can't endure the personal challenges this field forces upon them. While many businesses and industries rely on a multitude of sectors, facts, and figures, the direct sales business is arguably the simplest of the lot. You get sales and you generate revenue; you build a team, and they generate revenue…that's it!

Despite it being that simple, it could arguably one of the toughest ones in which to truly succeed. However, with the right guidance, knowledge, skills, and mindset, it really does hold the potential of changing your people's lives in ways you cannot even comprehend. Take it from someone who has witnessed the power of direct sales firsthand, me. It works, and it can be extremely lucrative. Besides, if it wasn't, I probably wouldn't be writing a book about it.

I know what many of you might be thinking, "Why should I opt for direct sales and not some other business?" Or maybe you are thinking about building a team and want to know why other people in your network may find it a viable option for them. As it turns out, there are several reasons why this business is the one that entrepreneurs tend to love.

Entrepreneurs live and thrive on data. They need all the information they can get to make the most of the opportunity at hand. Here are some interesting numbers to share, just to showcase the potential of direct sales for anyone who might be considering starting their own direct sales business but was waiting for some kind of confirmation.

A 2017 report showed some data that an average of 74% of American people ended up purchasing a variety of goods and services from a direct selling company. As of the same year, the United States of America alone generated a direct sales revenue of $29.8 billion (Gaille, 2017).

Those are some really interesting numbers, and one can only assume just how massively this industry would have grown in the following years. Keep in mind that we are in 2021, which kind of sparks a bit of curiosity. Has the direct sales market grown, especially considering the kind of situation the world is going through? As it turns out, yes, it has. It has almost doubled in market capacity, with a jaw-dropping $55.0 billion of revenue pouring in. The market is further expected to grow by a mouth-watering 1.2%. Now, that may not seem enough, but when you put into perspective the billions of dollars, that is a massive rise (IBIS World, 2021).

The direct sales business is a type of entrepreneurial endeavor that has the potential to create the life that you want for yourself and your family. Whether you are seeking a second or third stream of income, or you want to build something that you are proud of, that your family and friends can be proud of for you, this channel of sales is for anyone. Maybe you are looking for freedom to create more choices for yourself, or the ability to finally stop worrying about money. Anyone can succeed here… it is the great equalizer. Why? Because it is direct sales, sales directly to the consumer are done through network marketing. Meaning, you are marketing and selling to *your* network. Your network is made up of people who know, like, and trust you. People buy from people they know, like, and trust.

The beauty of a direct sales business is that anyone can jump in and get started. Of course, it does go without saying that if you have some experience in sales that's an extra bonus and could go a long way. However, if you are someone who has no idea about sales, do not worry. All you need is determination, energy, focus, and a system, a plan of action. The *Direct AF Sales* is my brand, my identity, and through it, my purpose is to help people build and access their own directness, grit, tenacity, mental toughness, resilience, discipline and courage. I know I have the tools in this book to teach you how you can empower yourself and those who join you in business, frankly, any who is trying to find a way to change themselves and their approach to building their business.

And if you are worried that you don't know how to recruit the right people, what kind of system to operate, or even how to sell... don't worry... I've got you! There are challenges that all of us have gone through, and there still will be some that we may face. There will always be challenges, distractions, and disruptions. Always. We are going to accept the hurdles, obstacles, and problems that all of us have and build a business anyway. For now, understand that it is perfectly okay to feel slightly overwhelmed, but it is not okay to let those feelings derail you or stop you from taking action. If you are someone who has been searching for answers, trying to find that one way that can help you achieve so much in life, and have something that you and your family can be proud of, you are on the right track. With a bit of push, you could just be the next big thing I might be reading about somewhere soon.

Here is the thing...to become a lawyer, a doctor, an engineer, you can access textbooks and other resources that serve as manuals. In each of these fields, you find yourself plenty of resources to learn from and draw lessons from. However, when I entered the direct sales business, there was no manual. There isn't a one-size-fits-all kind of document that you can execute to perfection. There are a million things to consider, such as the team you are working with, the product or service you are selling, the profit margins, the operation itself, etcetera. I had a blank slate, and because I was so busy, I had to invent the wheel that rolled for me and be the visionary of my venture. Therefore, I decided to put together my system that helped me train candidates and recruits the way I wanted. That system was originally just a document that I called the Five Daily Steps and it served as the foundation of the entire direct selling business for me. With time, I refined it, honed it, implemented it and trained on it. Soon, I was having success, and so were the people who were using that system on the regular.

Naturally, other people both in and outside of my little team became curious and asked me what I doing to have such early and fast success, what was I was saying, what was my system… what did they have to do and say to make things work for them. Bear in mind that many of these people were not on my downline, meaning their success would have no impact on my business, my growth, my income or my success. However, I fully KNOW IN MY SOUL that there is *unlimited opportunity for growth and wealth* in direct selling. There is room for everybody! The possibilities are as wide and deep as the oceans. There is tremendous wealth that can be created and there is *__enough for all__* of us! Therefore, whether someone I help or teach makes me money or doesn't make me money, it doesn't matter! I am here to serve as many people who will accept and implement my help!

One way to reach a lot of people was to put my system and method into a book. Immediately, I questioned myself "Who am I to write a book? Who am I to train people?" I had only been doing this for a few years. I started writing this book in early 2018. I picked it up and put it down a million times but when I went on to achieve the highest title in my direct sales company, my power and accountability partner reminded me I had reached the goal I had given myself and I could now finish the project. Those two things gave me the push to feel confident enough to finish the book and put it out into the world.

The idea behind "direct AF sales" is quite simple; no BS, no excuses, no blaming, no focusing on failure, and no worrying about what other people might think. Just be straight to the point with yourself about your own level of activity and with your network. There is no reason to be anything other than direct and simple or to overcomplicate things. Another way of saying be direct and straightforward is to say be honest with yourself and your network in the way you communicate. Working only in truth and reality, aka being straightforward and direct, can often be intimidating and challenging for some, and yes, it may be challenging and uncomfortable at first, but that is okay. Here is a truth you need to accept before we begin: **Not everyone is going to like you, not everyone is going to want to join your team, and not everyone is going to want to buy your products**.

I want you to succeed. There is enough for all of us to succeed at a big scale. Someone who holds themselves out to you to be your friend/coach/mentor/leader is doing you a disservice if they aren't telling you the truth. No one in direct selling is going to give you a trophy medal. Trophy medals and cheerleading might stroke your ego for a short period of time, but they will not help you build a sustainable business. However, someone who tells you a hard truth that might temporarily sting is a more caring and more loving mentor because he or she is giving you the tools that you can use to build a thriving business. Would you rather have someone speak truth to you that might be uncomfortable to hear but will lead you to your ultimate success or would you rather have someone tell you what you want to hear, but you stay in exactly the same place you are and never reach your goal?

What's right is right and what's wrong is wrong. If you choose to run your business by hearing only what you want to hear and staying comfortable, you will not reach your goals. I want you to succeed so I can't sugarcoat the truth. I am here to help you learn what it takes to enter the business and how you can go on to excel in this field, creating a network and utilizing all your efforts and resources properly.

With that being said, I know how hard it can be to start your journey into this incredible and challenging world of direct sales. *Direct AF Sales* is here to guide you on how to plow right through challenges, know what you need to know, and fine-tune your focus on what actions you need to take to produce results. Through my stories, I intend to share lessons that you can walk away with, apply to your own business and get the most out of. I do not hold back, so buckle up buttercup.

Okay, that's enough with the introduction – time to get down to business!

Chapter 1

From a Prosecutor to an Entrepreneur

Fear is an emotional reaction.

Courage is a decision.

One of the wonderful things about network marketing is that people who are in this business come from a variety of backgrounds and all walks of life. The perception appears to be that it is often daunting for people to jump directly into this profession, and perhaps that is because that some people are afraid or intimidated by the idea of selling. Sales, let's be honest, is not something everyone can get worked up about until they learn and truly understand the incredible power the direct selling channel actually holds.

My path into network marketing was anything other than direct. I didn't go to business school nor did I have sales experience. Hopefully, someone finds something in my story that they can relate to, and can benefit from hearing it. All of life, the good and bad, the ups and the downs, happens for you. Your circumstances and experiences create who you are.

My open and honest approach may stem from with the fact that I was born in Brooklyn and raised in New York. Maybe most of it has to do with the fact that I worked as a trial lawyer for 21 years. By profession, trial lawyers have to face the facts of their case head on. I had to acknowledge and embrace all the facts of a case as they were, the good, the bad and the ugly. Trial work forces you to address the good facts that support your theory of a case as well as shining a spotlight on those bad facts that kind of maybe hurt your position too. I had to simplify complicated scenarios, and through learning those skills, I became a very quick thinker and concise analyzer and communicator.

For anyone who has been in criminal trial work, they can understand, empathize and relate to my experiences as well as the way I communicate. We trial lawyers are a special breed who love the trenches, a fast pace, thinking on our feet, asking direct questions of witnesses, and leading witnesses on cross-examination to extract the facts that we need for our arguments. I didn't learn to be simple and straightforward; I developed and strengthened that muscle over time.

Helping People

Like most teenagers and young adults, I had zero clue about what I wanted to do with my life when I grew up. As I write these words now, I can vividly recall the moment that all changed, that one fateful day in high school during a study hall where I came across a *Time Magazine* issue that was lying on the top of a table. It immediately caught my eye among the pile of other newspapers and magazines. On the cover, I saw a very young woman cradling a baby in her arms. It wasn't the sweetness of the baby or the emotion of the picture that caught my attention; the young woman's arms were black, metal prosthetic limbs with hooks instead of hands. (This was mid-1980's so prosthetic devices weren't as attractive looking as today). I knew I had to read the article to find out what had happened to her. I raced through the article, and as I did so, my heart just broke. Here's what happened: when the girl on the cover was only 16 years of age, she was hitchhiking through Florida. A guy pulled over to give her a ride. She hopped in and they took off. Soon, he pulled over on the side of the road. He dragged her into the brush, just off the highway. There, the guy raped the victim over and over again, sodomized her, and then chopped both her arms off and left her to die. This survivor, this iron-will young lady, crawled out of the ditch on what was left of her arms and onto the main road. Bleeding, gasping for air, desperately looking for help, she was ultimately rescued and brought to the hospital. As a result of the rape, she became pregnant and decided to have the baby.

The atrocity, the cruelty and the heinous nature of the crime, well, it just ripped me apart. It made me furiously angry. I knew right there that I could fuel this energy into serving and helping victims of crime. I decided I would become a prosecution. I wanted to be the person to punish those who walk God's earth freely, without fear or regret, thinking that they can get away with anything. I wanted to make sure that people were held responsible and accountable for the wrongs that they committed against others.

From then on, my journey was as focused and streamlined as a train on a track. I went to college and studied political science, concentrating in law and legal issues. I went to law school and volunteered in the victim services office and as a volunteer student prosecutor. I graduated, passed the bar in California, and got a job as a Deputy District Attorney.

Side bar: by the time I got to the Orange County District Attorney's Office in 1997, I discovered that one of the women who worked in the clerical department was the survivor in the rape case featured in that Time Magazine. The very same person whose story directed the course of my life up until that point worked in the same office with me.

Life went on and after a few years, my then husband, our new baby son and I moved back to the East Coast. Upon arrival, I learned that there were no jobs available for prosecutors as most of the offices were on a hiring freeze.

For a short time, I was able to find some contract work, making appearances in court for various civil attorneys. It was the worst…I hated it. Let me tell you, civil attorneys aren't all that civil compared to criminal defense attorneys. Anyway, one day, sitting in Woburn District Court, waiting for the judge to call my case, I met a woman and we struck up a conversation. She had gone to law school to be a public defender. We talked that day and the next. We exchanged numbers and we grew to be extremely close friends. To this day, we remain close and of course she is a customer in my direct selling business. I told her my background and she told me that the state public defender's office was hiring. I couldn't imagine myself being a defense attorney, defending people who had been accused of committing crimes. Truth is, I despised the work I was doing, and my family needed money. And I missed criminal trial work. So, I kept an open mind and I applied to the state's public defender office.

Becoming a Public Defender

Soon after, I landed the gig and was now a criminal defense attorney. At the time, the office only handled felony cases and sent the misdemeanor (the less serious offenses) to be handled on a contract basis with the private bar. That meant I was going in deep, right away. My first case that I was to handle was a three-defendant gang-rape and sodomy case. Wow! What a twist of fate. For someone who had become an attorney for the sole purpose of ensuring that people who had committed crimes were held accountable, this was quite a situation I found myself in. Now, I had to defend the accused. I had to go to the jail to interview my client. To say I was horrified would be a massive understatement.

I sat at my desk and went into autopilot. First thing, I had to get through reading the police report. Here's what the reports told me: three guys, one being my client, apparently grabbed a young woman from the side of the road as she was walking and drove off with her. She said that each of them raped her, and two sodomized her. They threw her back on the road without her pants or underwear, and she was forced to walk home.

Right about now, my stomach was in knots and I was kicking myself for choosing to move and take this job. I forced myself to get up and walk over to the jail so I could go interview my client. While I was waiting for the guards to bring my client to the interview area of the jail, I felt nauseated by the stench inside the area. The air was stagnant, heavy and I felt sick. I had no idea what to say to my client. The guards finally got him there and he sat down just a few feet away from me. His wrists were shackled together as were his ankles. We started talking and what happened next changed the entire way I viewed the world.

His story was diametrically opposed to hers. He told me that he knew the girl from high school, that they all knew each other and had agreed to meet up. That she was bored and lonely with her boyfriend away in the military and that would have sex my client and his friends. I didn't believe him. And then he told me that the girl video-taped the entire thing. That the videotape was with his brother. He told me to go get it and watch it, that it would prove his innocence. And it did.

That case, for me, was a gift from God – To open my eyes, not make snap judgments, to teach me that there is no white or black; there's just a million shades of gray!

My client was telling me the absolute, God's honest truth. The video revealed beyond any shadow of a doubt that the young lady was enjoying consensual sex with the three young men, that they drove her home and waited until she had gotten inside her house before. Absolutely nothing resembling the truth was in the police report that I read, and of course, the case was dismissed.

Side bar: I am still in touch with that client today and his former fiancé ended up joining my direct sales team as a brand ambassador. How's that for crazy?

So How Did I Wind Up In Direct Sales?

By the end of 2005, I had four children all under the age of 4. I was working part-time in the public defender's office and things were H A R D financially. My then husband and four sons moved back to Orange County, California because as public defenders here, we would each earn enough to support our family. Of course, this meant that we both worked full time and needed a nanny.

Time went on. My then husband and I ending up divorcing and that meant less time with my kids. They were becoming teenagers and I knew something had to change. I needed to find a way to create more time freedom, more balance and be home more with them. One day, as I was complaining to a dear friend of mine for the *umpteenth* time about finding work that would enable me to spend more time with my kids that I could do in addition to law, she told me about one of *her* new clients who was killing it in network marketing. I was like, "what's network marketing?"

I had no idea what network marketing or direct sales was, nothing about sales, nothing about the company that the other girl worked with and after hearing more I was a HARD NO.

"You want me to sell stuff?"

"Just listen. She goes on all these wonderful trips, she earned a fancy car…they are always sending her gifts…just go and talk to her."

"Yeah…. I don't think so. No!"

This went on for a couple of weeks, and every time we met, my friend encouraged me to consider it. I would always turn down the suggestion. One day, that lady whom I hadn't met so far decided to leave a sample of what she sold for me with my pal. The product was just amazing, and I knew I was going to order some from this woman so I texted her and decided I'd meet up and hear her story and see what it was all about.

My main goal was to figure out how much money one can make in direct sales. If it was something that could supplement my law income, meet my expenses and keep my financial situation in good standings, I was in! It was just one sample, but in a leap of faith, I decided to give it a go.

The next day, I met with the sample lady. She went on to show just how limitless the earnings could be. She shared details about her first paycheck, how she goes on to earn, and all the things that I wanted to know. To be honest, I felt like "if she can do that, I can do that!"

Figuring Out the Details

When I started this business, I "knew" in my gut that it was a scam and that I was going to fail. I mean, here I was, a woman in my mid-40s, a lawyer of 21 years working full-time, and a mom of four sons. These kids were in three different schools so that meant I was driving them to 3 different locations before heading off to court to get my cases called. When I said yes to joining a direct sales company, I hoped that it could create some extra income so that I could take fewer cases and be home with my kids more before they finished growing up. I had no real idea of what I was getting myself into since I had no sales experience and didn't even know what an MLM was at the time. But I knew that I wanted to create some extra income so that I could create some time freedom and create some balance in my life that didn't yet exist.

In April 2017 I started my journey into network marketing and joined a multi-level marketing company. I told my sponsor that I would give it 60 days and all she had to do is tell me exactly what I had to do. So, in my first month of business, I just did exactly what my sponsor suggested that I do… tell people about my new business and have an in-person event to share information about the products I was selling. I was quite hesitant because I didn't want to have house parties to peddle product to my friends, but I was coachable and did it anyway. I quickly realized that there were only a few things I could do to grow my business, and endlessly posting on social media about my products was NOT one of them. Within the first six months of my business, I created a simple and efficient system that I could do before work in the morning, during the breaks in my day, and before bed and my business grew. And grew quickly. And that method is the one I am teaching you in this book.

Chapter 2

You Actually Can't Start with Your Why

You Actually Must Start with Your WHAT

In his September 28, 2009, Ted Talk, Simon Sinek discussed his discovery that he coined "The Golden Circle". He identified that there was a pattern among the great and inspiring leaders and organizations, like Apple, Dr. Martin Luther King and the Wright brothers. Sinek asserted that these leaders inspired action by starting with *why*; that Apple, Dr. King Jr., and the Wright Brothers are all leaders who think, act, and communicate the same way which in complete opposition to everyone else, i.e., the Golden Circle… why, how, and what. Sinek stated that very few people or organizations know why they do what they do, what their cause is, their belief, their purpose, and why their organization exists. Inspired leaders all think, act and communicate from the inside out. And therefore, he asserts, people don't buy what you do, rather, they buy why you do it. For example, in their marketing, Apple communicates from the inside out. They start with their why, explain their how and then reveal their what…the product. Sinek then brilliantly goes on to explain that our human brains are organized in the same way as the Golden Circle.

He says:

"None of what I'm telling you is my opinion. It's all grounded in the tenets of biology. Not psychology, biology. If you look at a cross-section of the human brain, looking from the top-down, what you see is the human brain is broken into three major components that correlate perfectly with the golden circle. Our newest brain, our Homosapien brain, our neocortex, corresponds with the "what" level. The neocortex is responsible for all of our rational and analytical thought and language. The middle two sections make up our limbic brains, and our limbic brains are responsible for all of our feelings, like trust and loyalty. It's also responsible for all human behavior, all decision-making, and it has no capacity for language."

Make no mistake, Simon Sinek is brilliant. But in my humble opinion, when it comes to ordinary people trying to start and build a direct selling business, "starting with a why" isn't the way to move forward, move into action and stay in consistent, daily activity. I know, this might raise quite a few eyebrows but bear with me on this one.

*You do not need a why, you need a **what** to start or grow your business, your journey towards success.*

Starting with why as a leader or company, to inspire people to buy your product because they don't buy what you sell, they buy why you sell it… they believe what you believe is Sinek's point. When Apple makes a commercial or an ad, their copy is appealing to your limbic brain, the portion of the brain responsible for all of our feelings, like trust and loyalty. Our limbic brain is responsible for our behavior, our decision-making, and it does not have a capacity for language. It's based on emotion, feeling, and gut instinct. Our limbic brain responds to our why.

Our neocortex, our Homo-sapien brain, corresponds with our "what" level. It is responsible for our rational thought, our analytical thought and our language. As entrepreneurs, we must rely on this, our neocortex, to pinpoint our "what" to be able to develop grit, resiliency, discipline, tenacity and to be able to build a business that will succeed.

If we rely on feeling, emotion or even worse, motivation, our business is doomed. In other words, if we rely on our limbic brain to stay in consistent daily action (which is what is required to build a business), if we rely on our "why", our businesses will not thrive. People who rely on their why rely on whether they feel like working on any particular day, they are not consistent, they don't follow a system, and they stop and start their businesses to death.

What I am suggesting is that we rely on our **what**, on our neocortex, on the part of our brain that is responsible for rational thought. Each morning, by relying on our what, on our neocortex, on our rational decision-making portion of our brain, we can make the decision to work our businesses, whether we feel like it or not. Whether we are motivated or not. Whether we are feeling under the weather or not. The neocortex part of our brains tells us that if we don't work our business today, it will not grow. It's the same part of your brain that tells you to get up and go to your 9-5 job when you don't feel like it.

Soon after I started my network marketing business, I achieved some kind of rank increase and therefore got to be part of a three month long exclusive training led by some of the finest trainers I have come across to date. One guy in particular said a few things that really resonated with me then, and even now. He used to say, "When I think about my business and work my business, I don't want or need a "why" that makes me cry, I just want a house cleaner." He went on to explain how he and his wife were both working, his wife working as a nurse during the day and he at night. They had kids and that naturally meant that he was with them during the day and she at night. There was always so much to do and keep up with and at the time, all he wanted was to make enough money to be able to afford a house cleaner and make things just slightly easier.

Once that first goal (his what) was achieved, he needed a new what so that he could move forward, continue to grow. His next "what" became earning enough money to be able to have his wife begin to work part-time. Once that was achieved, it became another new what: this time he wanted to grow and earn enough so that he could drop down to only part time work as well. His goals, his "what" continued to change as he went on to achieve every one of those milestones he set and slayed.

*It is your specific, tangible, definable **"what"** that will push you into, and keep you in action, not an amorphous, intangible, nonspecific **"why"**.*

In many direct sales companies, including the one that I work with and love with my whole heart, one of the first things new consultants are coached to do is to discover our "why". In other words, we are taught to find out why we are

40

starting our MLM business. We are told that successful business owners who identify and connect to their why, their reason for starting their business, will help them create clear goals and make a plan which in turn will help them overcome obstacles. Specifically, forming a plan helps create a vision for your future and that vision can be considered your "why". Your "why" is your reason for building your business, an attempt to keep you motivated and focused. Your "why" is meant to inspire you to move into taking the action(s) that will grow your business. Your why is your north star, what guides you, what moves you forward, what you can fall back on when you become lost or slip up in your biz.

The MLM company that I am a brand ambassador with has a worksheet to help us uncover our why. One of the first questions on the worksheet, with space left blank for us to write out our answers, is "what do we want to change, enhance, or accomplish for ourselves and/or the people around us" as we begin to identify the goals that our business can help us achieve. Another question is "who are the people in your life that could be affected by you having more flexibility and financial success?" And this is an excellent question to consider because the truth is that the people in your lives are a key part of why we do the things we do, whether that's starting a business to create time freedom or flexibility or stopping for groceries on the way home from work to create a healthier meal choice for our loved ones.

41

Because let's face it… going to work for a company is relatively easy compared to being an entrepreneur. If you go to work as an employee, your motivation to show up every day is because you need to keep your job, you need to be paid, you want a stable paycheck and you don't want to get fired. Things like needing food, money for your rent or mortgage, your health insurance, well, these necessities in life tend to motivate you enough to get up every day, go to work, and do a decent enough job that you don't get fired. Right? Being an entrepreneur means you have to be self-disciplined, self-directed, focused, encouraged, and positive because you choose to be. If you aren't feeling motivated and don't work on your business, you're not going to get in trouble, or fired. Unless you yell at yourself or fire yourself, which isn't productive. So, it does take a special kind of person or personality to start your own business, especially one in direct sales. The truth is that it isn't easy to stay motivated in direct sales, to accept all the "rejection", to work hard, and not see a lot of return right away. The majority of people quit, quite literally. They either terminate with their direct sales company or they just stop working their business and dabble a bit here and there.

Understand That It is Imperative You Know Your 'What'

Let me be crystal clear: having a why isn't going to hurt you. It is not a bad thing to have. But don't fool yourself…. It is NOT enough. It is not going to be enough to make you get off the couch, turn off Netflix and move you to work in a sustained, long term, disciplined and consistent way. Even the most solid why might give you a little push, some motivation, but that's about it.

Vision boards have become all the rage, particularly in the direct sales community. Put simply, a vision board is a physical manifestation of your goals, hopes, and dreams. Many truly believe, including me, that creating a vision board is *so much more* than cutting out images and ideas from magazines and pasting them onto poster boards into an inspiring collage and then hoping for the best. It can be a powerful and wonderful way to identify your aspirations and begin to put the law of attraction into practice.

In fact, Mel Robbins has said that the brain doesn't even realize the difference between a visualization and a memory. Visualizing what you want to achieve, whether it is a title, an income amount, a car, a house, a trip, whatever… the act of visualizing sets into motion your ability to achieve them. The continuous process of seeing it in your mind's eye or on an actual vision board somewhere in your home or office sets of new neuropathways in your brain and your mind reverts to that which is most familiar. So make your visualizations what your brain wants to think about and revert to. Visualization plus action is the law of attraction being put into proper use.

Now, with all of that being said, all of this is good and important to remember and to do. But visualization or vision boarding without consistent action is nothing than day-dreaming. Visualization without consistent action is not going to build you a business, a team, or a solid base of customers. This is important here. None of these things are going to make you money. If you started your network marketing business and making money is not your primary purpose, then you can stop reading here and just carry on with your life. But if earning income is one of your big goals and reason why you went into business, then let's put on your big boy or big girl underpants and get real.

This system that I created is a system that has absolutely NOTHING to do with my "why." I honestly would rather just put in the work and move on with my day whether I'm feeling motivated or not on any particular day instead of remembering my why, having a good cry session, and then pulling myself together before I feel motivated enough to send messages to five people inviting them to learn about my amazing side gig. The last and most important thing I'll say about your why is this: it is never going to be big enough or emotional enough to make you develop the habits, skills, consistency, grit, or mental toughness that it takes to work your side business every single day. It is only by relying on your neocortex, your what, that will build you the success you want and deserve.

Set SMART Goals

Business students, I know you will identify this right away. For anyone who has no idea what a SMART goal is, let me quickly explain. Any goal that is specific, measurable, attainable, relevant and time-bound, is considered a SMART goal. To give you an example, if you say your goal is to be rich, that is a bad goal. Instead, if you were to say, "I wish to earn $1 million over next two years," now that sounds like a goal because:

- It is attainable – provided that you figure out the right way to do it

- It is measurable – You can count the money that you make to figure out how far you have progressed

- It is time-bound – That deadline means that you will always have a time limit, hence the natural push to work more

- It is specific – It describes exactly what you are chasing

- It is relevant – Most likely!

Here's my suggestion: if you are new, or you need a reboot, aka, kick in the pants, simply start with your what. What does that mean? A small, bite-sized, attainable goal. Ask yourself; what do you WANT from your business? Time freedom... too tangential. In my former life as a trial attorney, I would have said to you...

Objection... Vague!

Meaning, you can't define that. You can't put an end date on that. It isn't specific enough. That's joining a gym and saying that your goal is to lose weight.

Objection... Vague!

You've made it too easy on yourself to fail. How much weight do you want to lose this month? You need a specific, targeted, and definable goal that has an end date where you can measure whether or not you have achieved your goal, just like I mentioned earlier. Then you can examine the work you did or didn't do to achieve or not achieve that defined goal. If you did lose the specific amount of weight in the allotted time and you are happy with that progress, set that same goal for yourself for the next month. You'll know exactly what you need to do to achieve it and you can repeat the behavior that led to the result. If you are happy and feeling encouraged by your progress, you can improve upon and increase the level of activity and behavior that got you your result. If you are unhappy and didn't achieve the result, you can look back and examine what went wrong, where it fell apart, what you did or didn't do, and either adjust your behavior for the following month or not.

Same with your business. If your goal is to generate $500 in business in your first month, then that is your WHAT. Ask yourself if your goal is big enough to push to you act on whatever it is that brings you closer every day to achieving your goal. So, for example, I didn't set a goal until my second month in business. As I said, I was surprised at how much my first check was when compared to how little time and effort I put into it. I decided to set a goal that my second check would be double my first. That was my first WHAT. It was small, defined, and it was super attainable. I understood that if I increased my effort, and my output, then I would likely meet my goal.

Let's go back to the losing weight analogy for an example. Your goal is to lose weight and that is a good and meaningful goal. But it is not specific or defined. And therefore, because it's not specific or defined that means it gives you an easy out. Don't bad habits feel good right away? Isn't it so fantastic to eat the fries because they just taste so good? Anyway, because it is not specific or defined it means that there's no way for you to measure your success. Or failure. It also means it's super easy to quit and give up on that goal.

But what if we changed that just a little bit to make it more definable and we broke it down into more of a bite-size piece. What if we altered your goal to say that in your first month you wanted to lose 5 pounds. That sort of specific, attainable, and a defined goal would give you, or your trainer at the gym, a much easier way to help you reach your goal. Now, he or she will teach you the steps that you need to take at the gym, which machines to use, how many days you need to show up, how many repetitions to do of each exercise, maybe even how many calories you need to take in each day and so on. It is more likely that with the bite-size goal of a five-pound loss in one month, you will see progress from your action, and your belief in your ability to lose weight will increase. When your belief increases, your output of action increases even more. Which leads to an even firmer belief in your ability to reach your goal. And so on.

Take action first, and your belief will follow.

Let's translate this back to your business. Please do not tell me that your goal is to build a team. Simply saying that you want to build a team is not defined or specific. I would much prefer if you told me that you would like to recruit two new team members per month so that you can build a kick-ass team. Oh, now that's a whole other story, isn't it? Now, I can tell you exactly what kind of output you need to execute to achieve the goal of recruiting two new people a month!

Side note: Don't wait until you achieve your goal to assume the role, or the title, or the identity of whatever your goal is. Let's assume for the moment that your goal is to quit smoking. Assume the identity of a non-smoker before you quit. Identify yourself as a non-smoker. Become that person mentally and adopt that person's behaviors. What does a non-smoker do? What do they act like?

Ok, back to business. Let's revisit the weight loss example and let's say your goal now is to lose 50 lbs. Move into the action to begin losing the weight but in your mind and in your actions, become the person you imagine yourself to be 50 pounds lighter. That person may carry themselves a bit differently, more confidently, more self-assured. Maybe that person takes the stairs every day instead of the elevator. That person eats differently than you do now. Do the actions, the things, the behaviors that a person who has already achieved the goal you want does.

In my direct sales company, I wanted to achieve a certain title. I decided in my first year of business to conduct myself as if I already achieved it and ran my business accordingly. A person with the title I wanted did not waste time scrolling through social media, or daydreaming, or thinking about what they *might* do to build their business. A person with the title I wanted had to spend about 80% of their time allotted to their direct sales business working their own business first and then 20% working to help their team. A person with the title that I wanted had to recruit new business partners and made sure they got new customers and exhibited all of the behaviors and actions that they wanted to set for their team. A person with the title that I wanted had to outperform every person on their team to show the way. A person with the title that I wanted had to constantly learn how to do new things that would help grow their business without waiting for someone to tell them to do it, who took risks and made hard decisions, and had tough conversations with people.

Creating Discipline

Despite what I had come across, and everyone telling me how I should seek out my 'why' that would make me cry, I preferred to stick to a discipline of my own that let me get the shit I needed to get done to grow my business and then move on with the rest of my life. I am normally a disciplined person, and I am only competitive with myself. And that ensures that I do not need someone or something external to motivate me. I am reliant on the neocortex portion of my brain when it comes to my how I work my business. I decide to do whatever it is that I do. For example, I do all my exercise at home through a streaming program. I don't need a trainer or to go to a scheduled class to force myself to do what I enjoy doing. Most people, however, need external motivation to do the right things. These are the people who need a constant reminder of why they are supposed to do what they are supposed to do.

An extremely easy way to start to create discipline in your life is to start with the small stuff that seems unimportant. It's paying attention to details in life that you don't think matter. Consistently focusing on the same, small, seemingly insignificant tasks create a person who will carry that discipline into the bigger areas of her life. For example, start with the tiny details of just doing the right thing. Make your bed every day, wipe the toilet seat after you use it, return the shopping cart, pick up trash and throw it out, even if it isn't yours. Do the right thing when you are presented with the opportunites.

Here is another way: create a power list. Write down 5 critical tasks to complete either before going to bed for the next day or first thing in the morning. 5 critical tasks are small, attainable action items that you are in control of whether they get accomplished or not. The tasks must be attainable, measurable, relevant, time-bound and specific.

For example, a critical task list could look like this: call two people, follow up with 4 people, make one appointment with so and so, post about x on social media and go for a run. You are in control of whether or not these tasks get done. Here is an example of what NOT to put on a critical task list: recruit 1 person, sell product to 2 people, publish a book…. These things are outside of your control. See the difference?

If you create and execute on a critical task list every day, by the end of the year, you will no longer be able to recognize yourself or your business because you will have developed an incredible amount of momentum in your action, belief in yourself, the product and the business model, confidence, grit, tenacity, resilience and discipline.

Now let's look at motivation. If you were to rely solely on motivation, what do you think would happen? Motivation is dependent upon your current state of emotion, how you feel at any given moment. If you are in a good mood, maybe you'll focus on your business. If you are sad, confused, scared, I don't think you'll feel motivated to work your business.

Motivation is a fair-weather friend who also happens to be a giant ho. She is a C-E-HO.

Relying on motivation to start, grow, and sustain a business is as good as relying on a fair-weather friend to be there for you. She just isn't there for you consistently. Sometimes she isn't there for you when you really need or want her to be. Relying on motivation means you are going to stop and start your business to death. Stopping and starting your business to death kills your self-esteem, confidence, momentum, and your credibility disappears. The more stop-and-start you do, the more inconsistent you are, the faster you will fail. You lose credibility with your network but that isn't the worst of it. You will lose credibility with yourself.

The best thing you can do to cultivate good habits and create discipline is to tell motivation to piss off, step into your greatness now, assume your success has already happened and that you don't need permission from anyone to grow into your best self. You are your pacesetter; you are walking the walk and you are powerful.

Take a look at this excerpt from a Ted Talk given by Christine Carter called "The One Minute Secret to Forming a New Habit":

*"**The goal, remember, is repetition. Not high achievement**. So let yourself be mediocre at whatever you are trying to do. But **be mediocre every day**. <u>**Take only one step but take that step every day.**</u>"*

Every action you take is a vote for the person that you want to be. Chief Executive Officers read self-development books, take initiative, challenge themselves, continue to grow and learn… Actions and habits are a way that you can embody the identity of the person you want to become. Action isn't the same as motion or even busy-ness. There is a clear division between the two. Action is something you do that gets results. Motion is related to action, but it won't get results.

Chapter 3

Method and Mindset

"Action cures fear"

David J. Schwartz,
author of The Magic of Thinking Big

Which comes first, the mindset or the method? Belief or action? The method is the how-to and mindset is the why-to, and if you want to build a successful network marketing business, you can't have one without the other. Here's the problem: Methods, aka systems, are boring and repetitive and mindset work can be scary or intimidating. You're getting out of your comfort zone to do boring, repetitive work. What? Are you asking yourself if you read that right? Yes, you did. Did I mention that I am going to be brutally honest about how to be wildly successful in direct sales? We are going to do what no one else is willing to do; we're going to dig into the minute details that every other book glosses over. Because that's where the magic lies, the daily method that will create your unstoppable mindset. And if you master this, success is inevitable.

Learn How to Learn

My parents instilled in me a very, very important piece of life lesson which I have passed on to my sons:

Learn how to learn, so that you can always take care of yourself

One of my core values is being a life-long student. I always strive to learn more so that I can continue to grow. Initially, it might have not meant much to me, but now it makes all the sense in the world. If someone would have taken my bar license away, how would I support myself? When you have the skill of knowing how to learn, you are always capable of leaning on yourself, depending on yourself and going into something new successfully. If the direct selling company that

I work with decided to shut down tomorrow or move into more traditional retail selling, what would happen? Would I panic and think my life was over, that the sky was falling? No, of course not. I'd be disappointed and sad because I love what I do, but I would be ok. I would learn something new and adapt. I'd find another adventure.

One of the very important lessons that I was taught, as a young child, was the value of working in order to earn something that I wanted. If I wanted to go to summer camp, I would have to earn half my tuition fee to join the summer camp. Now remember, I had all year between summers to do just that. The way I would "earn" was to perform chores around the house like cleaning the kitchen, cleaning the bathroom, sweeping, cleaning out the garage, doing yard work, etc. There were slips of scrap paper in a stack on my Dad's desk in his office and I would write down what chore I did, how long I did it for and my rate. In other words, I was billing much like lawyer would do for their time. I gave my Dad my little billing stacks at the end of each week and he would tally it all up for me in a log he kept. I started this at age 8.

This would go on week after week. Some weeks I worked a good amount and some weeks not at all. That was ok, because remember, I had from September of one year to May of the next to come up with half the tuition for the summer camp. I was never paid in actual cash; my hours and total pay were kept in a log on his desk. So, we were able to track my progress and I learned how to gauge how much I would need to do in any particular month. My first year I was able to not only make half the tuition and get to go to summer camp in upstate New York for 8 weeks, but I also learned the magical art of padding my billing time. You know, like if I worked between 15-30 minutes you round up to the half hour…. Come to think of it, I'm surprised I went into criminal law where there is no attorney billing. I probably should have gone into civil law, where there is massive padding! I knew what I was doing when I was 9 for goodness' sake!

Anyway, another important takeaway from this is something we all need to apply to our businesses which is this. Start with your end goal. What is it that you want to accomplish? In my example, I needed to earn let's say $1000.00 for half the camp tuition. (I'm making that number up to illustrate the point because I really can't remember what the tuition amount actually was, and the actual number isn't really relevant). But I do remember that it was a lot of money, so let's say it was 1000.00. Knowing where I wanted to go made it easy to plan out just how I was going to get there. I had 10 months to bill out $1000.00. I was allowed to bill at $1.00 per hour that I worked (it was 1979 after all). So, I would do the work, write out my little billing scraps of paper and proudly leave them in a stack on my Dad's desk for him to go through and enter into the journal.

Now, as an adult I realize there was no way a child of 8 actually billed 1000 hours of housecleaning in 10 months. That wasn't the real point of the exercise. At the time, I thought I did earn all that time. My parts likely entered whatever into the journal and threw the scraps away. The lessons my parents were teaching me were not about actually earning the exact dollar amount. The lessons were about the value of money, the value of hard work, the importance of working consistently over a long period of time toward something that you really want, the importance of discipline, of keeping track of your time because your time is a commodity and worth something, and so on. Pretty fucking amazing, am I right?

Imagine if you were to set a goal right now of what you want to achieve in your business. Set it out in a defined period of time, for example, 6 months from now or a year from now, you will have achieved the goal you are setting. When you can master that kind of mindset, training, and a taste of the real world, you work backwards from your goal

My Mom and Dad instilled the "what's the worst that can happen" mentality in me as well. I remember talking with my Dad on the phone toward the end of law school. I had to decide my next move and whether I was going to take the bar in Massachusetts or California. I told him that I knew for sure I didn't want to stay in Massachusetts, but I was scared to pick up and move across the country. The Massachusetts bar at the time had a high pass rate and was only a two-day test but California was the hardest bar in the country and a three-day test. I just didn't know what to do even though deep down I wanted to move to California. Instead of telling me what to do, he asked a few questions. He asked what I was afraid of. I said, "I'm afraid of failing, not passing the bar exam, not getting a job..." He said, "How do you know unless you go and try? Just try... what's the worst that can happen?"

Makes sense, right? You never know until you try. That mindset has since stuck with me. Not a lot of people get that kind of mindset from their parents, and I am grateful that I did.

In everything, absolutely everything, mindset matters. In life, in relationships, in self-care, and in business. Particularly in the direct selling channel. Mindset is such an important topic that it can be an entirely separate book in and of itself. This book, however, is where I am going to show you how to simply, efficiently, and effectively implement a technique called the Five Daily Steps or "the method". If executed properly and consistently, you will see transformation and success. It is a blueprint, a step-by-step, guided approach to "doing the things" that are going to bring you success. "Doing the things" are called the "IPA's" or Income Producing Activities that will grow your team, increase your sales and fatten your paycheck. The Method WILL help you reach your goals. The thing is this: if your mind ain't right, then absolutely nothing I tell you in the rest of this book will be helpful because you won't move into action.

Mindset trumps skill set every single time.

In other words, you can have all the skills, all the knowledge, and all the tools in the world but if your mindset is not on point, if you are frozen by fear, you won't move into action, or do the things, or implement the skills you learn at all. And your business will not grow. It will fail.

Your mindset dictates how successful or unsuccessful you will be in your business. If you are feeling excited and confident and ready to shout about your business and its products from every rooftop anyone will let you shout from, then you will be successful. Because you will move into action and do the work with enthusiasm and positivity. And that is what your network will respond to. And be drawn to.

You started your business in direct sales for a reason. Maybe you are a full-time 9-5 worker who is sick of feeling stuck and wants a way out of traditional corporate America. Perhaps you love your full-time job but want a second stream of income, a Plan B. To save for the upcoming vacations you dream of taking, or for college, or to pay off student debt. Or are you a stay-at-home mom "SAHM" who is seeking out community, an outlet for your creative energies, to satisfy an urge to do something for just yourself? Whoever you are and whatever reason you have for starting down your multi-level marketing path, you have got to get your head in the game and run your business like a business and not a hobby. The truth is that you really can achieve your potential and more through an expansive mindset and enhanced activity.

The First Step

One of the first things I want you to say, out loud, right now is: *I am not smarter than the system*. Repeat it. *I am not smarter than the system*. You may be absolutely brilliant and incredibly successful. But you aren't smarter than the system. Right now, you are fresh and open and ready to learn no matter how brilliant you are. What I'm going to teach you in the pages to follow is *a system*. If you choose to follow it, great. Give it a minimum of 90 days of daily, consistent effort and see what the results are. But for the *love of Jesus*, please do not pick and choose which of the steps within the system you are going to "like" or "feel comfortable with" or choose to do. Please don't pick one step and ignore the other steps. Please don't say, Oh this is great. I love this method. I'm going to do steps 1, 2, and 3 but not 4 or 5. Yeah, that's not going to work. That's like going on a diet and liking part of the diet but not the other parts of the diet and deciding which rules of the diet you are going to adhere to and which ones you are going to ignore and then when you fail to lose any of those pounds hanging on, any of that weight that bugs you so much, you will complain to anyone who will listen that the diet just doesn't work. You will blame the diet, not the fact that you didn't actually follow the diet.

So, don't be all up in my grill in a few weeks telling me that you tried my method and it just didn't work. Umm… I'm going to cross examine you until the truth is revealed: that you simply didn't follow the method as prescribed for a long enough period of time.

It's Okay to be Uncomfortable

I can guarantee you that there are parts of this five daily system that you are not going to like. There will be something that makes you feel uncomfortable, that will put you outside of your comfort zone. *That's ok.* It is ok to feel uncomfortable or unsure and do it anyway. There is no growth where there is no discomfort. You won't die. You won't pass out. You may be nervous or fearful or anxious. That's ok. Do it anyway. You've got to force yourself to do it. If you need help, reach out to someone to ask for help. But do it. Whatever it is that is making you uneasy and want to stop in your tracks is what you MUST do. And after you do it for a few days in a row, it won't feel bad or uncomfortable anymore. It will become routine, easy and you will feel nonchalant and ambivalent about it. Facing your fears, overcoming them…that's where the good stuff is. That's what makes you a badass, a leader, a success; that's what personal growth is all about!

One of the biggest obstacles you will put in your own way is your resistance to being coachable and not being open to the system. You must decide to be coachable. You must adopt the mindset that you have decided that you are going to work your business, you are going to be consistent. You are going to be disciplined. You are going to touch your business every single day, even if it is for 30 minutes. Even if that 30 minutes is spread out over 12 hours. You get to decide. You get to be in control of you, of your mind, your habits, your priorities, and your behaviors. I recently got a message from someone on my downline who has been inconsistent and barely working her business. She had her first event the other night. She messaged me saying how much fun it was and how it re-inspired her to work her business. She finished her message by saying "I just wish I didn't go back and forth so much." Seriously? See where I'm going with this? Who is she wishing helped her? She has the power to control whether or not she goes back and forth or whether she can be disciplined and consistent and strong. She gets to decide this. So, this is a woman who isn't working her business consistently not because she can't, but because she hasn't chosen to. She hasn't decided to. She hasn't committed herself to it.

Sorry, Not Sorry... We Must Revisit the Concept of Motivation Again

Let's talk finish addressing the elephant in the room. Not only is feeling motivated all the time unnatural, but it's particularly difficult when you face the consistent and constant rejection from your network… the no's, ghosting, and sometimes, even the downright nasty replies! And I don't care whether you are brand new to networking marketing, like haven't even started your business yet or whether you are an OG, and have been around slinging for over 10 years.

Now, everyone with a heartbeat has good days and bad days. Some days you are positive, feeling happy and you will be super motivated. Some days are blah, bleak, sad, or you're just plain tired. You don't feel like doing the things. No one on earth is motivated all day, every day, seven days a week. So, the reality we need to face is that you simply cannot rely on motivation to work your business consistently. And if you don't work your business consistently, you will fail. Take for example one of the most common New Year's Eve resolutions that people make… joining a gym and getting in shape. It's a new year and people are feeling motivated to get going and finally lose that weight. And we all know what happens, don't we? People start strong! They show up that first week, nice and early, ready to rock and roll, maybe even

65

show up at the gum for a full five days out of that first week. The second-week hits, and maybe they hit that snooze button, or they feel sore so they decide that they did so well the first week, that they can skip a day and hit it tomorrow. By the third week, they are down to maybe once or twice a week at the gym, and come February, more than half have fallen off. Motivation, that fair-weather bitch disappears when the going gets tough. And trust me, friends, the going WILL get tough! So, what's a network marketer to do, you ask? Time to why that amazing 10 letter word is the true, dependable pal and that word is...DISCIPLINE.

Discipline – Your Real BFF

Marine Corp Aviator fighter pilot David Burke spent 23 years as an elite fighter-pilot and he understands that motivation is meaningless. "In Hollywood, the home team wins the game thanks to the coach's inspirational speech, and the troops hold the line thanks to the general's heroic sermon," wrote Burke. "In real life, when fear, fatigue, and doubt set in, no speech can provide the motivation you need to keep going. The only thing you and your team can rely on is discipline." No "why" you are doing this business is enough to simply motivate you to work. Burke states, "Discipline is cherished in the Marine Corps. We cultivate it in everything we do, from how we fight to how we dress, cut our hair, and clean our rooms." Now retired, Lt. Colonel David Burke now sees that "discipline also provides a template for what businesses should identify and develop in their employees. More than any other quality, discipline is what drives a person to succeed when faced with adversity. And that's what the real world is: adversity".

"Discipline", Burke continues, is what "drives you to do the work you don't enjoy, but is required. Discipline conquers fear. Discipline keeps you going when your curiosity, motivation, and excitement evaporate."

Discipline is defined as training to act in accordance with rules, activity, exercise, or regimen that develops or improves a skill, the rigor or training effect of experience. Executing the five daily steps exactly as prescribed, each and every day for a minimum period of 90 days to start will absolutely help you develop that discipline muscle. The longer you do this Method, the stronger your discipline muscle will become. When you have discipline with respect to working your network marketing business on a daily basis, your mood doesn't matter; whatever is happening outside of your business becomes irrelevant to whether it will produce the work that needs to be done to move your business forward.

Jim Rohn, who mentored industry giants like Tony Robbins, says that "it takes consistent self-discipline to master the art of setting goals, time management, leadership, parenting, and relationships. If we don't make consistent self-discipline part of our daily lives, the results we seek will be sporadic and elusive. It takes a consistent effort to truly manage our valuable time. Without it, we'll be consistently frustrated. Our time will be eaten up by others whose demands are stronger than our own. It takes discipline to conquer the nagging voices in our minds: the fear of failure, the fear of success, the fear of poverty, the fear of a broken heart. It takes discipline to keep trying when that nagging voice within us brings up the possibility of failure. It takes discipline to admit our errors and recognize our limitations". He also says that it takes discipline to change a habit and to plan. Discipline is super easy to talk about and extra difficult to cultivate, learn and implement, no doubt. But nothing worth doing is easy. Let's get after how we develop discipline.

One place to begin is baby steps. And that is precisely the reason why The Method is broken down into five baby steps that you execute every single day, hence, the five daily (baby) steps. Big, drastic change is hard for us. Think of that New Year's resolution of hitting the gym five days a week on January 1st. Going to the gym consistently five days a week for a year is drastic and difficult and the majority of people quit. People just simply burn out and revert to more comfortable, known behavior. Slow, simple, and steady is the best place to cruise. An article in Wisdomination is spot on when the author says,

"When you progress in baby steps, you will find yourself a new person a year hence, not knowing precisely when or how it happened. The trick here is to make a small change and let your brain accept it as the new baseline. This will make the next step easier because the baseline moved. Wash, rinse, repeat… What I'm gonna say now may sound banal, but it really isn't: Big things are composed of small things. Small changes that you stick to and follow every day add up to surprisingly massive results."

Consistently performing The Five Daily Steps will not only build your business, but it will develop the qualities that all top entrepreneurs possess: a discipline which in turn develops grit, resilience, determination, perseverance, courage, mental toughness, confidence, and self-esteem. The longer you do the daily steps, pushing past the first 90-day window, the more you will cultivate real grit, real tenacity, strong perseverance to succeed, to win, to get to where you want to be, and beyond. Once you develop and strengthen these traits, the more tenacious and unyielding you become, you will be unstoppable. The word no will mean nothing to you. It won't stop you. There will literally be nothing that gets in your way. Except maybe yourself if you even allow that. You will be successful the moment you decide to be. Adopt the NOPO (No Other Possible Outcome) mindset around your own success: there is *no other possible outcome other than you winning.*

Chapter 4

Step One: Create Your Master List

Get clear on your vision by starting off organized

Starting Your Daily Steps

The very first thing you need to do is to create a master list. As you begin, clear your mind of any judgments or any preconceptions that you have of the people that are in your network. Please stop deciding for the people in your network whether they want to hear from you or not hear from you about your products or business. Think of someone you know, who is in your network. Are you already prejudging them, deciding before you write their name down on your master list whether they are a good or bad candidate for your business? Or are you assuming that you know what's actually happening in their lives?

Get a pen and a notebook and just start writing names down without thinking about what they do for work or if you think they have enough money and don't need a second stream of income, a side hustle, a Plan B. It is not up to you to decide if the person needs or wants the business opportunity you are about to present to them. You don't get to pretend that you are psychic, that you can read minds, orthat you know what is best for them. Just write their name down. You will be shocked at how many people you know. And you will be shocked at who actually says yes that they were looking for a Plan B.

The list will eventually be well over 800 people – think of every area of your life… college, graduate school, high school, your current full-time job if you have one, middle school, elementary school, Facebook, Linked In, Instagram, Twitter, your neighbors, church, temple. Be open to anyone. Remember to include in your list family, people you know in your community, people in your phone, or in your planner. Here is a list that will prompt you or trigger your memory:

Accountant	Actors	Apartment manager
Art Instructor	Bank tellers	Barber
Baseball coach	Basketball coach	Cell phone contacts
Chiropractor	Choir	Church
Coaches	Coworkers	Dance Instructor
Day Care worker	Dentist	Dental Hygienist
Dietician	Doctor	Dry Cleaner
Editor	Electrician	Estheticians
Family members	Fire personnel	Florist
Former Boss	Former Co-Worker	Former Roommate
Friends	Golf friends	Grocery store
Hairdresser	High school friends	Hockey team
Holiday Card List	Interior Decorator	Landlord
Librarian	Makeup Artists	Manicurist
Massage Therapist	Nurses	Office Manager
Orthodontist	Parent's Friends	Pediatrician
Pedicurist	Periodontist	Pilot/Airline Stewards
Police Officers/Staff	Professors	Realtors
Secretary	Single Dads	Single Moms

Son/Daughter	Spouse's network	Stepchildren
Spa owners	Teachers	Waiters/Waitresses
Workout Partner/Gym Owners		

Think of your job as being a professional inviter. You must invite people to learn more about your business and your products. Your list will be initially everyone you've ever met or known, and you will add to it as you progress into your business. You will meet new people in all sorts of ways, as long as you put yourself out there. And if you are in network marketing, you have to build your network. By putting yourself out there. You can meet people through your children, but also by joining clubs. Every connection you make, every person you meet could be an opportunity to share information and build your business. You've got to force yourself to get into the habit of listening for opportunities in conversations you have with people where you can offer information and invite them to learn more about what you do. Here are a few ideas to get you thinking, but just do a search on Google or Facebook and you'll come up with lots of other ideas for yourself.

- Book Club
- Golf Club
- Bridge Club
- Lions Club
- Rotary Club
- Toastmasters
- YMCA
- YWCA
- Bowling League
- Basketball League

Consider networking through your Alumni Association, Facebook, LinkedIn, Twitter, Instagram and Clubhouse. Eventually, you are going to feel like you've literally run out of people and you've been working your same list for so long and you are tapped out. What do you do? MEET NEW PEOPLE! We are in an age of social media and virtual communities, so go mingle! Join groups that interest you whether in person or online. What are your interests, your hobbies, something that you have wanted to learn? To build and expand your network.

Remember that as you go along in your journey that you cannot forget step one of the Five Daily Steps. Keep working and reworking your Master List. You've got to consistently add to it. We will talk about how to grow your network and add to your list throughout the book, particularly in the social media chapter.

If it makes you feel more comfortable, start with your "dirt list". The dirt list is comprised of those people in your network that love and support you so unconditionally that they would buy dirt in a bag from you if you sold it.

Don't avoid your chicken list. These are the people that you are terrified to approach for whatever reason that you created in your mind about your perception of them.

Make sure to include your social media list. These are the people who you follow and who follow you on social media. Your Facebook friends, your Instagram followers, your Twitter followers, people you know on WhatsApp, people you have met through Clubhouse, your Pinterest contacts. All the social media, go through your lists with a fine-tooth comb and add them to your master list.

Add all of your cell phone contacts. If you have a spouse or a partner, be sure to include their cell phone contacts as well.

Find all of your education contacts. Think about your college roommates, high school classmates, graduation class, fraternity brothers, sorority sisters, alumni groups, college major associations, professional groups. If you have a spouse or partner, remember to include their contacts as well.

Finally, your customers. Don't rule out your current customers, former customers, retail customers, and of course, potential customers.

Chapter 5

Step Two: Reach Out + Invite People to Learn More

Leading with Your Business Opportunity, AKA, The Fast Track

Let me give you some cold and hard truth. Prospecting and recruiting are literally the heart and soul of direct selling and network marketing. Around 99% of the people just do not want to reach out to their network and lead with the business. They don't want to do it because they think or have been led to believe that this is scary and hard. They do not wish to go through the struggle, they don't want them to become pushy, and they do not want to be the person others would avoid, just because this person constantly talks about something they are not interested in. They don't want to be "that girl". If you want to grow a big business quickly, you must sponsor people and build a team

You have one main job here and that is to get really, really good at inviting. You don't need to be an expert at anything in your direct selling business except for being an expert at inviting people to learn more about what you are doing with your business and your products. So many people are afraid of being rejected, of being turned down or facing a blunt 'no. The reasons I train on this are simple:

1. You are planting a seed, an idea that they may be capable of doing this too, and

2. You are complimenting them – I love what I am doing, maybe you will too. I think highly enough to you to ask you if you want to take a look?

What you must remember is that you are not pushing, forcing or convincing others to do something you want them to do. Rather, you are offering a **_gift_** of an opportunity and the possibility of an additional source of income. Do you knanyone who wouldn't want some additional money pouring into their accounts every now and then?

"The only people who are not in network marketing are the people who simply don't understand it".

Jeff Altgilbers

The truth is, and I tell my team this as well, that 99% of the people you offer business to will say 'no' or they will ignore you because they may not know what to say to you in return, yet. This is normal and it is nothing to be alarmed about. Most people aren't sitting around waiting for a message from you asking them if they want to start a business. Your message probably took them by surprise. You have to give them a minute to consider the idea. You've planted the seed of an idea with them, and now your job is to water that seed and see what, if anything, grows from it. The truth is their immediate response, or lack of a response doesn't matter in the long run because your first reach out to a prospect is just the beginning of the process.

Here is the language that I have used. Please don't waste your precious time trying to craft the perfect or magical combination of words that are so incredibly compelling you will have people knocking down your door ready to join your team. The formula I'm giving you it is tried and true. It works.

Please don't alter the format of it because you feel uncomfortable or unsure about using it. Trust the process. *Repeat to self: I am not smarter than the system.* Here is what you want to say when you

"Hi xxx (Insert name)! Hope you are doing great! I'm so happy I started my business with (insert which direct sales company you are with). It has done incredible things for so many on my team and I'm excited to see what it is going to do for me. I think this could be a good fit for you as well. If I sent you some information, would you check it out?"

Now if you are new, you'll want to stay with the invitation format above. After your business does actually begin to do incredible things for you, you can say that. You can change it to something like, "My side gig is doing incredible things for me." And continue on with the rest. But it's important to **_be completely transparent, authentic and open_**. If the business has not yet done anything wonderful, never exaggerate or lie about it.

The goal is to keep your invitation to learn more about your business straightforward and simple. Another goal is to make it sound like YOU, not me. So here is the basic format of any business opportunity message can be broken down into a formula:

- A greeting
- A friendly, courteous statement
- A positive statement about your business or how you feel about your business
- A statement planting the seed that your business opportunity could be something that would fit into their life, do something positive for them, etc.
- And finally, end in a question… If I sent you something to read, would you take a look? Or, if I sent you some information to explore, would that interest you?

THAT'S IT! Use the formula above to craft a direct, straightforward, friendly, nonapologetic message for your prospects.

If the person says no thank you, that is okay! Please do not take it personally. The fact that they didn't accept your invitation to learn more about your business has absolutely nothing to do with you, how they feel about you, how they feel about your business, or anything other than the fact that at this moment, they just aren't interested in hearing more about your new business. Tell them that you understand and that you want to get your great products into their hands. Ask where you can send a sample of the products that you sell. There are only *3 possible responses* that someone can give you on your business opportunity reach out.

First Outcome

First, and most common, is that the person you messaged will ignore you, aka, ghost you. In other words, you've text messaged or voice messaged a prospect, and they simply just don't answer you.

- Don't panic!
- Don't get upset!
- Don't assume the worst!

There are a million and three reasons why the person hasn't responded to you and none of them have anything to do with you. But when you first begin using this technique, it's natural to feel afraid because being vulnerable is hard. It is ok to be vulnerable. Your network will appreciate you more for your vulnerability and connect on a deeper level with you. So, let's talk about vulnerability and how you're going to need to **feel it and move through** it.

There is power in vulnerability because in that space there is room for growth. You must allow yourself the freedom to be vulnerable. When you reach out to someone, it feels like you are putting yourself out there. You feel as if you are offering yourself up. If the person you are reaching out to ignores your message or says no to your offer of information about the business, then it feels as if the person is saying no to *you*, to your friendship, to your value, to your soul! But this of course is not the case. Your prospect is just simply saying no to the information you are offering. If you reach out and offer a product sample and the person says no, again, they aren't saying no to YOU. Or no to anything about you. This vulnerability is created in your mind. As you begin to grow in your confidence in yourself, your confidence in inviting and offering information, your confidence in your business, and this business model, and your products, then you realize your vulnerability is not properly placed. Because this business is not about you as a person, a friend, a sister, whatever... there is no need to actually feel vulnerable.

Becoming unafraid is a process, a slow journey that takes courage at every new step. Courage isn't the absence of fear. Courage is the taking of action in the midst of fear. With each new action you take, every challenge tackled and conquered, confidence grows, and the skill of acting during the feeling of fear is further developed. Courage will be a byproduct of performing the Five Daily steps every single day for a minimum of 90 days because it will naturally grow from the confidence and discipline created.

Second Outcome

I spoke about this earlier in this chapter. The second possible outcome of your business opportunity reach out is that the person says no to your invitation, that they don't want to take a look at information about your business. They may offer a reason, and they may not. Most often, when someone says no, they say that they aren't into sales, or that they don't have time, just too busy, too much on their plate. So many network marketers try to then send another message that tries to counter their prospect's response. For example, let's say you reach out to Alice, and Alice responds by saying thank you, but not... I'm just not a good salesperson. Most network marketers are going to respond by saying, "OMG, that's what I thought too. I didn't think I'd be good either but it's so easy!" In other words, they try to convince their prospect that they are wrong. Instead of trying to argue with them or persuade them that they are wrong, just tell them that you understand and offer a free sample of the product that you sell and then ask for their feedback. "I totally get it... I'd love to send you some of my favorites and get your feedback... what address can I send some free samples to?"

Shifting from offering the business to offering the product instead of arguing with the person about how amazing your business takes enormous pressure off of your prospect and builds trust. You are in the job of offering information, not persuading or convincing people to join your team. Let your product do the selling, the convincing, and the persuading.

Third Outcome

The third possible response to your outreach is a yes, that your prospect does want to take a look at information about your direct sales company. I know how exciting these yes responses can be! Stay calm and send them some information about your company and what you do.

What do I send? ......

Send them information about your company whether that comes in the form of a newsletter, or an email, or a video from the company... there are endless pieces of information about your company that you can access from your company or your upline. You can utilize the power of a 3 way or connect call as well.

Leading with Your Product, aka the slow lane

There are some people reading this who just can't bring themselves to lead with the business. There are also some incredibly successful network marketers who have been in the business for a lot longer than I have who lead with their product. So please understand that neither way is the "right" way.

Some people who don't lead with the business are just too afraid, too uncomfortable, not yet ready to "feel the fear and do it anyway". Or maybe they just don't want or need to build as fast as another person might want or need. There may be some people in your network that you simply cannot bring yourself to reach out to with the business first, but you can certainly see yourself offering your product. For example, one of the best members of my team joined after I reached out to her with a sample of my product. Now, 9.5 times out of 10, I will reach out with the business opportunity first. But in this particular instance, however, she wasn't someone I knew well. We had never met in person. In fact, as I sit and write this book, we still have not met in person if you can even believe that! Anyway, we had never met in person, never spoken on the phone, and never messaged each other over text. I didn't even have her phone number when I reached out to her. My connection to her was purely online through social media. I have a very specific workout that I enjoy and I've been doing it for many years. There's an online group of women who also do the same workout and we support each other. It was through this workout method that I knew this particular woman. We followed each other on social media, and "liked" each other's posts, and sometimes may have even commented on each other's posts.

Anyway, on this particular occasion, I reached out privately through an Instagram message and offered her a sample of the products that I use and sell. Like most people, she graciously accepted my offer to send her a free sample. She sent her address and I promptly mailed out a few of my favorites. I followed up to make sure she received it. This particular woman didn't wait for me to follow up to see if she enjoyed the samples… she actually reached out to me to let me know how much she loved the products that she used (this is extremely rare so I should have known right then and there that she was a unicorn of joy) and asked me how she could order some products.

Tangent alert: Yes, I am a control freak, so I prefer when I can manage my customer's accounts for them but I also believe in excellent customer service and creating an exceptional customer experience. I suggest you do the same to create customer loyalty. Again, how you do the little things is how you do everything. Pay attention to the small details to create a discipline of striving toward excellence in everything you do.

Stay with the tangent for a second, because it will come full circle. Now, in my particular direct sales company, there are three ways to connect and purchase our products. The first way is to purchase our products retail. That means that you're going to pay full price, tax, and shipping.   The second way is to become a brand ambassador meaning you become a consultant and enjoy 25% off. The third and final way is to become my customer and receive 10% off. After my unicorn made her wish list of all the products she wanted to order, I presented her with all 3 of her purchasing options because that is in her best interest, not mine. She chose the smartest choice for her: the biggest discount. She fully disclosed to me that she never intended to share/sell these products with her network. She just wanted the deepest discount. After she began using the products, she began to talk about them. And that's how she started selling them. To this date, she is always one of the top two producers on my team.

There are a few morals to this story but for purposes of this particular chapter, the moral is that you can indeed lead with the product and still build a team. Someone may try your product and decide that they want to represent the brand as well as use the product and join before becoming a customer. But it is perfectly wonderful for someone to choose to become a customer of yours, and try the product, fall in love with the product and then decide later on at some point down the line that they have grown tired of referring their friends to you and would prefer to make the sale for themselves. Just because someone chooses to become your customer does not necessarily exclude them from your prospect list. Buyer beware; however, it is a significantly slower growth process if your main goal is to grow a team as opposed to growing a customer base.

Pro-tip: the more you embrace and accept hearing the word "no", the more you will grow. Use it as a stepping-stone to success. Meaning, if you reach out with the business opportunity and you receive a no, then you can offer a sample and grow your customer base. Your customer base is the low hanging fruit in your network so be sure to sporadically offer the business opportunity again to your prospect who then became your customer. You never know when that person may be ready to start *their* entrepreneurial journey. Just because they said no to you before becoming your customer doesn't mean they meant no forever.

Chapter 6

Step Three: The Fortune is in the Follow Up

The only thing you can control is how many people you put in your pipeline at one time and your attitude

The most recent information buzzing around inside the sales world is that it takes on average 10-12 "touches" or points of contact to close a sale. In other words, it takes the typical consumer 12 conversations or points of contact before they make a decision. And this holds true for whether the person is deciding to join your team or purchase your product. Please keep this fact in mind as you build your business one team member at a time, one customer at a time, one sale at a time.

As you send messages, make phone calls, as you reach out, you are doing what is called building your funnel. The truth is that you are in business. You are in the business of sales and a sale is a *process*. It's a process where the consumer is making a decision about whether they want to purchase your product or a decision about whether or not they want to join your team. Very rarely does someone hear about your business and join your team a few minutes later or even that same day. Very rarely does a consumer hear about your product and immediately purchase it, or even purchase that same week. When you introduce someone to *the idea* of joining you in business or purchasing your product, you are putting them into what's called a sales funnel.

The more people or prospects that you put into your funnel, the better off you will be and the faster you will move forward as you pursue your goals. If you aren't reaching out, then you can't build a funnel. If you don't have a funnel, then you don't have a business. The fuller your funnel, the faster your progress. An empty funnel means no sales, no one joining your team, and no growth. The more reach-outs you do, then the greater number of people are in your funnel.

Think about it like this: if you reach out to only fifteen people during one month, you will *maybe* have 3 of them in your sales funnel. Are you going to want to talk to the same

92

three people about the same thing? Or will you feel pushy and uncomfortable and bored? But, if you reach out to five people a day, five days a week, that is 25 people per week and 100 people per month. Let's say that's about 33 people or more in your funnel! How much more interesting and fun will that be for you? And that's plenty of people to talk with so you won't be nagging them, annoying them, pushing them, etc. Make sense?

Your job, after your reach out, is to move these people through your funnel as you *help guide them* into making a decision that is best for them. Not best for you, not what you want them to do, not what you think they should do, but to help them decide what it is that is best for them at this time in their life. Your job is to help them make a decision one way or the other. And the process of reaching that decision is normally an average of 12 touches or points of contact between you and them. But everyone's timeline is different. And we need to be patient with the process and the person going through the process. You are literally helping someone make a decision, come to the end or the conclusion of the process of learning about your business or product. Have confidence that no matter the outcome of one particular person, every step you take is a step in the right direction toward your goal.

Follow Up, then Follow Up Again!

You need to follow up after *every single contact* you have with every single prospect. As your business grows, your prospecting and funnel will grow. So, get organized. When you send someone a sample, make note of it, and make a system of when you are going to follow up with them about that sample. Hold yourself accountable to that date. It makes a huge impact on how your prospect views you and your business. It shows they are important to you and that you take your business seriously. Use what works best for you whether that is a calendar or an excel spreadsheet. Track the important information: the prospect's name, the date of your first reach out, how and on what platform you used to reach out. Was it a phone call, a text, a message on IG, a voice memo, an email? Keep track of whether the prospect responded, of the dates of all prior reach outs, the dates you plant to reach out again, and the date you sent a sample. Be sure to log whether your prospect received your sample and of course whether or not the person actually tried it. It's good to ask their opinion about it. Did they love it, like it? Your potential customer wants to know that their opinion of what you sent to them actually matters to you!

A common pitfall and reason why people fail or quit is because they spread that all-important follow-up contact, or touches, over a span of a year or more. If it takes 12 touches for you to turn a potential prospect into a confirmed sale, and you are following up once a month, it could take you a year to make one sale! You control the pace of your growth because you control the pace of your action. You can shorten the span of time between each of these touches or follow ups with your potential customer. There is no point in dragging it on to a year-long thing because truth be told, if you do it right, you could end up making a sale in less than a quarter of that time span, at the most! If you are really good, you might be signing up people on the second or the third touch, that too within a week or so.

Of course, I do want to clarify one thing. You are not here to nag the person to death, calling them over and over again to ask the exact same question "Did you try the sample yet?" That is ridiculous, and it is extremely annoying. Imagine yourself on the other end of the call and imagine how it would feel having the same person call you over and over again, and always asking you the same question in the same manner? You would be irritated, or worse, you might lose your temper.

There is a better way for you to do this. After your initial contact, and having the sample sent in, call them back a few days later and check if they have received the product. Upon confirmation, ask them:

"Great! Did you get a chance to try the sample yet?"

"Not yet!"

"Oh, I understand that you might be busy. Tell you what, I will check back with you in about three days."

What you have done there are two things:

1. You have shortened the length of time between your next touch and,

2. You have just planted an idea in the customer's head that it is worth trying the product, just to figure out what the fuss is about.

When you do not follow up in a shorter time, you tend to lose credibility with the potential customer. You also tend to lose your momentum, your passion, and your excitement. When the excitement fades, or when you take longer than a week or two, the customer automatically assumes that they are not important to you or that your business isn't that important to you, hence you are losing their trust, their confidence, and credibility in you and your product.

What really helps to ensure that you follow up properly is to use excel sheets, those big desk calendars, notebooks, et cetera. There is no point in trying to get something fancy, just go for something that works for you. If you are someone like me, you might prefer the big desk calendars that you can use to remind yourself when to call whom. If you are a bit tech-savvy, you can use a customized excel sheet.

The point I am trying to make here that you must work your business as a business. You are in the sales business where following up matters more than your initial contact. The warmer and quicker the follow-up, the more chances you have of making that sale. You must start treating your business as a business, and not just a side venture that you can work on when you want to. When you make your first call, you must know and understand that it will come with follow-ups that you will need to religiously adhere to and follow. None of this is hard. All you need is to be organized, and the rest automatically makes sense.

Don't Tell Me You Are Too Busy

Want to know a not-so-secret secret? When I started my side gig in network marketing, I was really, really busy so I forced myself to do my five daily reach outs from the toilet, first thing in the morning. I called it Prospecting from the Potty. I knew I had to reach out to five new people each day. So, in order to make sure I got my shit done (no pun intended), I woke up, immediately took my readers and cell phone into the potty, did all five reach outs and then, only after I got that crucial task done, would I go downstairs to get my coffee and start the rest of my day. I could perform the remainder of the five daily steps throughout the course of the day.

Whether you believe it or not, this is 100% true. I literally built my business from a throne, just not the kind of throne a king or queen sits on. The throne that **we all use multiple times a day**. If you are human being then you need to use the bathroom multiple times a day. That means you have multiple opportunities to sit down for a few minutes at a time and build a successful direct selling business. One trip to the potty at a time.

Side bar: Prospecting from the potty means you really need to have your master list in order. If you know in advance who you are reaching out to, then it expedites the process and keeps you organized. If you want to try Prospecting from the Potty and haven't yet made your list, just go sit down, go on to Facebook messenger and simply look for who is active. Then, click on their names, and if you haven't already sent them a message for the business, then go for it. Send it to five people, and then get up. Oh, and wash your hands.

In three minutes, I would be done with the entire day's work. To me, this had become a discipline for me, a part of my morning routine. This meant that I could drop my children at school, go to court, and pay attention to the rest of the day without worrying about a task that needed to be done. When I had to wait in court for my cases to be called, I would quickly check the messenger to see if anyone had responded. No? No worries there. I would simply check who I approached the day before. I would simply check and follow up with them.

I did this for so long that it felt like I was starting to run out of people. In other words, I felt like I had gone through my "warm market". I needed more people, and that is where the master list came to the rescue.

So far, my journey has been one that is brimming with success. I have many happy customers who know deep down that I care about them. They know I have their best interests at heart and they know that I will be honest with them and tell them the truth. One of the things I hear over and over again in every area of my life is that other people like that I say the things that they might only be able to think. They love my candor and my direct attitude. The fact is that I use the same mindset with my customers, and prospects, and in my personal life as well. The results just flow as a result.

Now don't get me wrong, I do want people to like me, but just because of that, I cannot change who I am, the way I act, behave or work. I am who I am, and my personality defines me. I do not hesitate to take on challenges, and I certainly do not hesitate to speak my mind. I am direct AF.

People often ask me if I really did go through my messenger while on the toilet seat, and I tell them the same thing; yes, I did. Leaving a message for someone doesn't need to be complicated. Except for the one time I accidentally

Facetimed one of the women on my team, Julie C., while I was on the potty, no one is looking at me or even knows where I am. Just do the work, get your shit done. And Julie, if you are reading this, thanks for laughing endlessly about this with me.

And don't pretend you aren't like every other human on the planet who has a cell phone and running water. The truth is people do take their phones and play candy crush or scroll IG stories when they go to the toilet. I am only showing you a way to maximize your productivity and (ahem) eliminate your bullshit excuse that you are too busy. If you tell me that you do not use your phone in the bathroom, that is totally cool. I believe you. Yes, I just rolled my eyes. You are missing out on an excellent opportunity to build your biz but you do you, boo.

(Just the) Tip to Remember

Be as direct and honest and real as possible in each of your follow-ups. People really do appreciate polite directness. You need to have a goal every single time you follow up, a purpose. Have a reason why you are contacting the person. Keep the follow-up about them, think about their interests, not yours. And, of course, end all of your follow-ups with a question. People, believe it or not, are still raised to be polite, and most people feel compelled to answer someone when they are asked a question.

Chapter 7

Step Four: 30 or More Samples Out a Month

Assuming that your business sells product, then you can perform the sample portion of step 4. Remember, you are reaching out to five new people a day, five days a week. That's 25 people a week, and if my math is correct that's 100 people a month. Taking into account that some people will ignore you, it's pretty safe to say that out of 100 messages, you will be able to send out or give out at least 30 samples a month.

I'm choosing to believe that YOU use, like and enjoy the products that you are selling. If not, why are you selling it? I'm choosing to believe that YOU believe in your products and that's why you are sharing them with your network. If my assumptions are true, then get samples out and let your products sell themselves!

If your company has prepackaged samples available to you to buy and then use to build your business, are you taking advantage of that? If not, why not? Take the time to build the relationship with your prospect or customer. Send the sample and be sure to send a *handwritten note or card* along with it, explaining what the sample is, what they can expect, how they use it, etc. This kind of extra attention shows your prospect or customer how much you care about them and about your business. Successful entrepreneurs go the extra mile, pay attention to the small details and do what other people cannot or will not do.

Take the time and have business cards made. There are hundreds of options online and on Etsy.com. Play with styles and colors until you find something that suits you. Put a message on your card, your name, phone number, website, directions on how to use your sample, whatever. Do these small touches, create momentum and maintain your consistent effort.

If your direct selling company does not have samples at all, and you cannot create any samples of your product, then all is not lost. Buy some of your product and host events where people can see, touch, feel, or try on your product.

Holding regular events either virtually or in person if you don't have the ability to share samples is a good alternative.

Chapter 8

Step Five: Social Media

Social media is a powerful tool you can use to grow your business, but it is not the source of growth. Notice that I put this as the final step in the five daily steps. That was not by accident. Social media is a great device for direct sellers but it is equally as dangerous. It has the potential to be a black hole that you can fall into and where you can get lost for hours at a time. It can be a diversion, distracting you from doing the things that are actually income-producing activities. It can eat up all the time that you allotted yourself to work your business. All that being said, it is a necessary and amazing tool for your business if used intelligently and appropriately.

There are so many platforms out there to use to connect and build your business. Social media is an incredibly effective way to build the perception you want people to have of you… aka "your brand". Your brand is what you want people to feel when they think of you. It's a space to leverage YOU, your personality, your quirks, your strangeness, whatever it is that makes your friends like the real you. The more authentic you are, the more you will grow.

Social media is your way to capture public attention, which is your advertising. You need to decide how you are going to present yourself and your business. It is your method of advertising. When you have a brand, running your business is easier. You want to use social media to encourage people to know, like, and trust you. People consume your product or service when they know you, like you, and trust you.

No matter what your direct sales business is, you need to remember what people are buying, what people want, and what people are ultimately looking for from you. People ultimately are buying happiness. People want to lose weight so they buy a product because that product will make them lose weight and ultimately be happier. People are buying the new CPA book on how to save more money in tax planning because they will have more money which will create more happiness. In other words, in some ways, it is irrelevant which particular product or service you are selling because the end result of buying the product or using the service will ultimately be more joy, more gratification, more happiness for your consumer. What you sell helps people become happier. So your message, your social media content must make people want to buy your product or service because you help them understand that you, your product, or your service can deliver more happiness to them.

Use it To BUILD Your Tribe

While the world continues to post pictures of how incredible their lives are or how they are having a super fancy meal at home, I am who I am. I can't pretend to be someone I am not. If I am happy, I am happy. If I am stressed, I am stressed. There is no reason for me to put on a façade and show people that I am playing a part or pretending that my life is something that it is not.

I am glad that I stay true to myself because honesty is another core trait that defines me. I use social media, for example mostly Instagram, to post pictures of my workouts. I post inspirational quotes, not just for me, but for the world to read and feel good. I post pictures of my baby girl dog Emma in all sorts of creative ways. I show that I a bit of a weirdo, a mom, a lawyer, and a housewife. I remember how people would tell me that I made them laugh because of the way I spoke, which was direct and funny. My Instagram is my true reflection. I still show the same side of me on social media, and that is what allows me to connect with more people. What they see is what they get. Simplicity and honesty!

One of the worst mistakes direct sellers can make is to incessantly post about their business. How boring! Your content needs to be crafted carefully. Be sure to stay YOU! And by that I mean, 80-85% of your posts should help your network show who you are, what your life is about, and what's happening in your world. The remaining 15-20% can be about your business, your products, your customer stories, your team, etc.

Be sure to post consistently on social media whether you use Facebook, Instagram, MeWe, Twitter, Linked In,Tik Tok, Pinterest, YouTube, or all of the above. There are apps available on both Apple products and Androids that you can utilize to make your life easier and schedule posts in advance. Be sure to post on your main feed, but also remember to use FB and IG stories! They are an amazing way to engage your audience.

Chapter 8

Accepting Reality

Nothing great is built from something that is easy. Nothing worth achieving stems from ease. Successful entrepreneurs don't shy away from hard things and we understand that progress takes time. There is no quick magic that will make your business win overnight.

For example, people who decide that they want to take up running don't just wake up able to run a marathon with 5-minute mile averages, right? I remember seeing this beautiful woman post on her IG feed showing the number of years it took for her to make progress in one particular yoga position. Her first photograph showed her at age 50, and in my opinion, her stance was performed pretty impressively! The same pose in the next photograph at age 51 showed some serious improvement not only in how much higher her right leg was able to go but also how low she was able to position her torso... I could visibly notice how much stronger she had become during that one year. The next picture showed her at age 52, the next at age 53 and the last at age 54! AND WOW! I was blown away! She had made such incredible progress and visible improvements in her strength and her power and her flexibility! Four years of repetition and discipline and hard work, and it showed.

I personally don't do yoga, but I have been consistently doing the Tracy Anderson Method for the last 7 years. And I truly believe deep down that performing the same type of workout for so long has enabled me to develop an understanding of what I am trying to convey in this book about discipline, consistency, resilience, and determination. Tracy Anderson has a few studios around the United States but also offers an online streaming service that someone can order monthly or annually. And every week, she offers 3 different classes: advanced, intermediate, and beginner. Entering this realm as a newbie, one would want to start with the beginner classes and learn the "language" that she is teaching us. As the months progress, and your strength, flexibility, and stamina increase, you can move on to the intermediate class. And then eventually the advanced. Once a week, Tracy has a conversation with her online streaming athletes about the workout, as well as other topics that come up. One of the things she talked about that stayed with me and made me think about the method that I'm teaching you was how one of the movements in her intermediate class was highly advanced. She jokingly reminded us not to yell at the screen, not to get angry or upset with her because she put in a movement that people at the intermediate level may find extremely hard.

She says that as she adds harder motions to help us evolve and grow stronger and until we are ready, modify the movement. "The permission slip to nurture yourself along the way is there. Don't attempt a move that is too hard and cuss me out" and give up, shut the computer and end the workout. Just modify. And since we do the same class, the same workout each day for between 5-7 days until she releases the new week's class, we are performing the same movements each day. This means every day you have a chance to attempt the difficult or challenging move and see if you can progress from one rep to 4. Or if you began the week by modifying a movement, can you attempt a few reps of the unmodified version by day 4? This is how you acquire new skills and shift perspective.

These are the lessons that can be applied to YOUR direct selling business as you incorporate the Five Daily Steps into your work. By day 30, if you begin to recognize that this method, this system is, in fact, actual work and that although it is simple, it doesn't mean it is easy… don't give up, don't throw in the towel, don't move onto some other magic system that flashed by you on your Instagram or Facebook feed! Don't yell at this book or curse my name because it has become challenging. NO! Stick with it, modify sometimes if you absolutely have to. By modify, I mean, don't do five new reach outs a day, do 2 or 3. But whatever you do, JNFQ!!!!*

JNFQ = just never fucking quit

This business is hard for the same reason that dieting or getting a six-pack is hard, or even parenting. Why? Just like in all these examples, you have to do things that you don't really want to do, just to keep the business alive. Like in the middle of the night, when you have a newborn and you don't want to get up but you know you have to change their messy diaper despite being dog-tired, you also have to do the same for your business. Most of the time, people really don't feel like waking up early, making those calls, following up, or sending the samples over, and if that is you, you simply won't see the success you want.

You are Worthy of the Success You Can Create

And just because something is tough doesn't mean it is impossible. The rewards that come your way far exceed any discomfort you feel when you justify every bit of effort you put into your business. If you really want to make your business work, find that need, that desire, that hunger and that passion to change your mindset. Be willing to do whatever it takes. You are worthy of the success you can create for yourself!

Fortunes are not made with ease, and every successful person has had their fair share of tough phases that they had masterfully maneuvered through. Challenges are a part of life, and the more challenging something is, the better the rewards are going to be.

I know someone who works in the direct selling business, and to be honest, she does not need to make any extra money. That lady is already very wealthy, but she continues to do it. I once asked her why, and she gave an answer that truly justified everything almost instantly. She told me that she does not have an identity beyond being a mother and a wife. She happens to be one of the highest achievers I know, and I see how happy it makes her. This business gives her that freedom, and that identity that she had been searching for. She is now a working woman again and someone's whose identity is no longer bound to the confines of her house. She loves what she does and loves having her work add to her identity.

Then, I have another woman on my team who found me on Instagram. We became friends on social media and after I built a relationship with her, I offered her a sample. I sent it; she loved it and she went on to become my customer. She started to order more for herself and began sharing information with her friends about her new products. When she messaged me to make another order, I offered her the idea that she could join me as a consultant. She considered the fact that if she joined the company as a brand ambassador she would enjoying the deepest possible discount on the products she was already using and loving. She made clear to me that she wasn't too sure if she wanted to or would even be able to sell anything. My core value of always doing the right thing meant having her join the team so that she could get the deepest discount. Getting the deepest discount was in her best interests and so she joined. Unsurprisingly to me, she told a few friends about it and began to grow a customer base. She has already brought a friend on to join her team and month by month, I'm watching her take a new step here and a new step there consistently. Her happiness is contagious! Now, she is selling, achieving, and she is one of the most disciplined people I have on my team! She is coachable, she shows up, and she loves what she has added into her life! Just to give you a glimpse of exactly how determined and self-motivated she is, she joined a zoom meeting immediately after a knee replacement while still being in the hospital! She is a cancer survivor, and that is saying something. I have seen her gain back her confidence and to me, that matters far more than anyone else getting a car or a massive paycheck.

Chapter 9

Direct Sales is a Journey of Personal Development

You and I both thought we were just starting a new business when we decided to join an multilevel marketing company. Now we realize that what we actually did was embark on an amazing journey of self-discovery and personal growth. Ed Mylett said it most perfectly:

"Here's the greatest thing about being an entrepreneur. The more you understand you, and get to know you, the better entrepreneur you are. Entrepreneurship is more about self-discovery and revelation than any other thing you'd almost

ever do in the world. Being an entrepreneur is actually the greatest personal development program with the highest possible compensation package attached to it of anywhere in the world, far more than as an athlete far more than as an actor or entertainer."

12/16/17 on the MFCEO Project

Taking on the five daily step system and incorporating it into your business takes courage, tenacity, grit, resilience, determination, self-esteem, humility, confidence, fear, the willingness to overcome, a desire to achieve and learn. Each sale you get, each business partner who joins your team is earned. You *can do* the work it takes, because you know that there is no shortcut to success. The five daily steps, done over the course of at least 90 days is going to keep you busy. So busy, in fact, that you won't have time for your old excuses, busy eliminating your limiting beliefs and scarcity mindset. You are in action every day and you are unstoppable! You are EARNING your success! Think about the word earn for a second with me. Here's how the dictionary defines it:

verb (used with object)
to gain or get in return for one's labor or service:
to earn one's living.

to merit as compensation, as for service; deserve:

to receive more than one has earned.

to acquire through merit:

to earn a reputation for honesty.

to gain as due return or profit:

Savings accounts earn interest.

to bring about or cause deservedly:

His fair dealing earned our confidence.

Here is an acronym for the word EARN that I want you to understand and adopt when you think about how you work, how you acquire each sale, how you are growing your grit and tenacity, your relentless determination, and resilience:

E: Effort

A: Action

R: Repetition

N: Non-Negotiable

Your business requires your effort, not your excuses. Effort means trying, and failing, and then trying again. The quote below show you what effort looks like.

"I've missed more than 9,000 shots in my career. I've lost almost 300 games. Twenty-six times I've been trusted to take the game-winning shot and missed. I've failed over and over and over again in my life. And that is why I succeed."

Michael Jordan

Action means doing the things every single day that are going to bring you one step closer to your goal, that will move the dial one click forward to you achieving the outcome that you want. Repetition means doing the same few income-producing activities that are going to bring about the desired results. It's ineffective for us try one system on one day and then switch to another and switch again on the third day. You have to do the same things over and over again not only until you master them and they become habits but also until they produce the desired result.

Nonnegotiable is the final piece. Entrepreneurs who maintain a mindset that their success is non-negotiable achieve whatever it is they want to achieve because they don't make excuses or accept the notion that they might not achieve their goal. Their confident mindset is firmly rooted in abundance, determination, grit, and tenacity and they will do whatever it takes to make it happen.

Move Forward

A woman named Allison Levine, a woman born with a hole in her heart, led the first all-female trek up Mt. Everest. One great lesson from her experience is this: if you aren't moving forward, you are going backward. This is so true for our profession! There is no middle ground. When you are climbing Everest, sitting still in one place can equal death. She understands that fear can be used to motivate you instead of letting it hold you back. It keeps you alert. Complacency on the mountain or in your business is dangerous. It can do you in. She understands that when you take on a challenge, push yourself out of your comfort zone and attempt to do hard things, you need to give yourself permission to fail and become "failure tolerant". You have to give yourself the freedom to fail, so you come back from it better the next time around. The only learning and improvement you can do in life are when you fight back from failure. So, you must feel the fear and push forward, move forward, and not become complacent.

Take Action

There is no magic trick, no secret sauce, no course you can buy that will get you to where you want to be because this business requires YOUR work. It requires YOUR action. It requires you to actually earn every single customer you get, every single consultant who wants to join your team, and every single dollar you make. You started this for a reason. There will be a million times that you get discouraged, frustrated, and feel like giving in. Every day something will happen that is going to discouraging but you have to keep going. It will build discipline and grit. You can't stay complacent if you want to grow. Don't be tricked into becoming complacent when you start to get momentum. Momentum can lull you into thinking you can ease up, slow down, or deviate from the five daily steps. As you continue into the days and weeks of utilizing the five daily steps, you are going to change. You are going to become more disciplined. Success utilizing this system will only come if you do it consistently for *at least* 90 days and exactly as prescribed. It's a lot like a diet or exercise program. It's hard to start and it's hard to stay disciplined but it will absolutely be worth it. Not only because you will see the results in terms of growing your business with new business partners and new customers, but also because your network is watching everything you do, especially with your business. Some of them are waiting and watching, sure you are going to quit, positive that you won't see it through, and that you are going to fail. The doubters will see your consistency and begin to believe that you are credible. The more consistent you are, for a long time, the more your network will respect what you are doing. And more importantly, the more YOU will respect what you are doing, respect yourself, believe in yourself and your business, all of it. You can't do the five daily steps every day for 90 days and not succeed. It's that simple. You will WIN!

If you follow this program for 90 days, every day, your network will see you winning. Once a few wins are under your belt, don't slow down, or stop! The five daily steps can and should be taken in 90-day increments. It can be easily taught to your downline, but only after you yourself have done it. You have to get in there, and sweat, and get comfortable being uncomfortable. Once you have been through it and see how powerfully effective this particular approach is, and you see for yourself the results you achieved, you will absolutely know who in your downline is actually doing the five daily steps and who merely say that are doing the five daily steps. One thing to remember is that *you will be on fire* and *actually enjoying the work* and you will then attract the people who also want to work, who you are inspiring. People will come and watch you all lit up on fire! Your action and your results and your happiness are going to get people's attention!

Your excitement is going to be contagious and your excellent results are going to draw a group of people, whether that crowd is potential business partners, potential customers, or a downline that wants to work with you and build something for themselves! Be ready because you will be inspiring other people that you may not realize you are impacting. People will gather to watch excellence, even if you aren't yet aware they are watching you. So, part of your messaging needs to be happiness and excellence. Keep this in mind when you are creating your content for emails, texts, newsletters, conversations, social media, etc. People want to smile, to laugh, want to be amazed, and want to be inspired. Let your abundance mentality shine through and create opportunities in all of your messaging to highlight happiness, success, stories of customer's happiness and success. It will be contagious! Is this always easy? No. Is it always convenient? No. But as Ed Mylett and Andy Frisella have taught me in the Arete Syndicate, "convenience and greatness cannot coexist. Convenience and excellence do not exist in the same space. The great things in your life that you are building are not convenient or easy. Easy is basic. Easy is common. Easy is not greatness. Difficult is special."

You are special. You are worthy of success.

Chapter 10

Why YOU Will Succeed When Most Will Not

If you want what I've built, then you have to be willing to do the work that I have done.

Direct selling and multi-level marketing companies tend to carry a bad reputation. Fortunately for me, I was oblivious to these rumors as I had no idea what direct sales or multi-level marketing companies were. It seems so silly that they seem to have a bad reputation as being a scam, a pyramid scheme, or that these companies are predatory and designed to suck people in when no one can really make any money.

Almost like direct selling companies are peddling hope or worse, actually doing something against the law. First of all, if MLMs or direct sales were a pyramid scheme, or illegal, then people would be put in prison and the company would be dissolved because pyramid schemes are illegal.

The truth is ugly and hard to hear but the majority of people do not make any real money in direct selling because they simply put no effort, time, or energy into their businesses and they have failed at it. It is THEIR fault and no one else's.

"Network Marketing is an untapped market because the majority of people who sign up don't actually work their business"

Ben Bethune, my 15 year old son

I am well aware that my words here may get me a lot of nasty emails but the truth is the truth is the truth all day long. If you don't work your business, you don't get a paycheck or a trophy medal. The majority of people will not get the paycheck, the title, the bonuses, the trips or the cars, or achieve any of the results that they want or believe they are entitled to receive. This chapter is going to talk about all the reasons why it is the PERSON who fails, not the direct selling channel. And why YOU WILL SUCCEED.

Here are the facts. 70% of the budding entrepreneurs who start are going to quit within the first few months of starting their business, that is, if they even get started in the first place. When I say quit, I don't necessarily mean they are going to actually terminate their independent contractor status with their company. I mean not work, not try, not sell, not network, not talk to anyone about their business, service, or product. Which by the way is why there are so many people not earning $1 on their company's annual income disclosure statement. If you took a moment to examine any direct selling company's income disclosure statement you would see that there are only a small percentage of people earning a reasonable amount of annual or monthly income. This is not because MLMs are a scam but because people aren't fucking working! Any critical thinker who understands this fact would realize that this is why these nonworkers are being included in the extremely misunderstood income disclosure statement data. One of the main reasons why is because they don't work their direct sales business *like a business* and *not like a hobby.* Meaning, they don't work it consistently, rather they work it when they feel it, almost as if it's an afterthought. These people rely on their why; they work when they feel motivated to work, which generally isn't often. Maybe they work for an hour on one day and then put the business down for a few days or even a week. Then they see or hear something that motivates them to work and they start again. They can't understand why their social media posts aren't bringing in tons of purchases, or why other people seem to be "better" at it than they are. Worse yet, they blame the direct selling model.

Another 20% of people will act, and be coachable, and put the effort in, but the minute something goes wrong, a business partner quits on them, or someone tells them no, or they take some kind of blow, their company does something they don't agree with, their belief will waiver and they will stop working. They will quit. They will dabble in their business and wonder why they aren't making money. Life will just simply derail them. Life is hard and it is easy to quit, and many people choose not to overcome obstacles.

The last 10% of people who start in direct sales are coachable and can roll with life's hard punches. They have a strong belief in themselves and their product, but they are not consistent and cannot act daily. The income producing activities are routine and boring and mundane. They get bored, they get inconsistent, and are unable to grind on a daily basis. Their fire has dimmed, their passion has dropped, they start slipping in their core values, they don't pay attention to the details, they make basic mistakes and begin to fade and slide down the slippery slope into failure. Into quitting.

A great analogy is to think about this: in most areas of life, a small percentage of people will be truly successful. Consider pro sports for example. How many kids grow up watching sports on television and decide they want to be a pro ballplayer. Probably hundreds of thousands. Naturally, their parents begin to get them involved in sports and they may play in school or in club sports. When they hit middle school, the number of players begins to tighten just slightly, and then by the time you get to high school, the numbers have dwindled pretty starkly. These kids have some talent and some discipline, and some will get drafted or picked for college sports. The majority of even these elite players will not become pro athletes. An extremely small percentage of very good, very talented people will make it to the big leagues. So, the big earners within MLM's are the very good, very disciplined consistent workers who made it to their big leagues so to speak.

Not Coachable

People fail because they refuse to be taught, guided, instructed and are not coachable. They aren't willing to be mentored or trained even if they have never had one day of experience in the direct selling arena. Even if they join you because they saw your success, they aren't willing to be humble enough to allow you to teach them what you do.

Unwilling to be Uncomfortable

They aren't willing to get uncomfortable. They want to take the path of least resistance. These people are too afraid to take action. They say well, so and so is better than me, I can't do what she does because… They are going to pretend to give effort and try but not really do anything except maybe scroll around on social media. For like, a week. These are the people that like to pretend that they are secret agents, carrying around a special secret that they can't share with anyone.

They are Success Zombies

"Success zombies" will not be the top earners of their direct sales company. They can't focus, they can't put into place one system and execute on that system for a long enough period of time to see if that system works or doesn't work. These people are looking for the magic, the quick fix, the trick, the tip, the secret sauce when the truth is that THERE IS NO MAGIC, THERE IS NO QUICK TRICK. There is only consistent, disciplined execution of the tasks that need to be done to move your business forward to achieving the goal you have set for yourself. I learned about "success zombies" from Andy Frisella in his MFCEO Podcast on October 5, 2015:

"One of these people who subscribes to every podcast, to subscribes to every book, who listens to every single person online, who reads everything they can, joins every program they can, goes to every speaker they can, and at the end of the day, they don't do fucking shit. That's a success zombie."

Now, he's not saying personal development and learning aren't important and wonderful, and neither am I. What I am saying is to learn but then you have to pick a system and actually execute on what it is you need to do so that you produce a result. You have to take what you've learned and put it into action. At some point, people need to stop moving around like a zombie, stop opening their wallet to every "coach" claiming success, quit wasting all of their time following around other people, and actually do the work. These zombies are in a trance-like state, looking for the next best trick, but never actually doing anything.

Lacking the Fire

These are the people who just aren't hungry enough. They don't have a good what. Success = action that produces a desired result. Over a long period of time. Cause and effect. Put work in and get a result. Not for a day, not for a week, not for a month, not for a year. Real success comes from long-term, repetitive action. Years and years of action, belief and momentum.

You will succeed because you are none of these things and because you have a system you can implement

Because you are doing the monotonous, repetitive income producing actions that are the Five Daily Steps, you are building your grit and tenacity and your wins are fueling the fire that will keep you going and attracting the right people to you. Importantly, not only do you have a system that works, you also have a system that you can easily teach to your team, to your downline and they can in turn duplicate it with their team.

You will succeed because you are consistently, on a daily basis, initiating new conversations with people about your products and business and you are building your network. You will reach your goals because you do not rely on motivation or whether you *feel like* doing the Five daily Steps; no, you rely on discipline!

Conclusion

Direct selling may or may not be for everyone, but it can be right for you. It truly is the great equalizer. Think of this... to jump in, there is a low upfront cost of entry, you don't need any fancy degrees or credentials, there are no specific education requirements to sign up. You don't need a background in marketing or sales. Things like gender, race, sexual orientation, gender identity, how old you are, how young you are, none of it matters! Anyone can do this! All it takes is determination, a desire to learn, a will to work, and a discipline that pushes you forward.

I'm so happy you read this book. I'm excited for you because you are now armed with all you need to absolutely slay your business. I realize that the five daily steps are simple and straightforward, but I also understand that the steps aren't easy to execute day in and day out, day after day, week after week, month after month for a minimum of 90 days. They can become a grind and monotonous. But you must take it in 90-day increments and when you are done with your first set, start again. Because what will happen is this: when you begin to see success, you're going to want to slow down, or ease up on the gas pedal. DON"T EASE UP when you become a winner! Why? Because one win doesn't stick around. As soon as one win happens, you have to move on and seek out the next. Wins are like motivation… they just don't stick around.

"Winning is a lover who takes you to paradise all night and then you wake up alone"

Tim Grover, author

The wins are super fun and feel amazing! But in the morning, they are gone. You don't want to be one and done. You want to KEEP ON WINNING! Stay in the game, keep grinding! And when you have reached your goal, built that team, achieved the highest title in your organization, reached the level of pay that you want, the desire to want to stop or worse go into "management mode" is going to kick in. If you succumb to that desire to stop or slow down, that will be day that will start the beginning of your descent.

The five daily steps, this system, this method, your entrepreneurial journey that you are on… think of it like a treadmill. Set your treadmill (journey) at a slow and steady pace. Slow and steady is something you can do a little every day. It is so much more effective in the long run for the health of your business to do a little every day instead of a ton on one or two days and then nothing for a week or more. Set your treadmill at maybe a zero or very slight incline so you that you don't strain yourself or pull something and set it at a nice slow pace of maybe a 1 or a 1.5. *Slow and steady.* If something happens in your life and you need to turn your attention away from your business, these settings (your mindset and pace) make it easy for you to quickly and safely hop off that moving treadmill and turn your attention elsewhere. And when you are ready to turn your attention back to your business and pick it back up, you won't have to get a running start to catch up with your business… you can easily pop right back onto that moving treadmill without any strain or struggle. Remember, this entrepreneurial journey you set out on is simply a treadmill that you've set at little to no incline, and a super slow pace. You've made that treadmill (your entrepreneurial journey) incredibly easy to stay on for the LONG HAUL. Well done, player.

You will have ups and downs, but the more you stay in consistent, daily, repetitive, correct action, the more wins you're going to be racking up in your win column. You're gonna get *real* used to winning… it becomes addictive. Your wins are going to be the fuel that pushes you forward more and more, learning and growing. Guys, there is literally no amount of money that you could pay me that would make me want to stop growing, becoming, creating, learning, and paying it forward.

Long term success comes from years and years of relentlessly building your direct selling business. There is no overnight success. Now that you know what it takes and how to do it, can you get yourself set up for success? Can you incorporate this into your daily routine? Fall in love with the routine, because this is the process of how you will win.

"Winning on a huge fuckin' scale is monotonous as fuck... this is the point...train yourself to love the day to day to day routine..."

Andy Frisella

My entrepreneurial journey in network marketing began as a side hustle that I felt was sure to fail. But everything that happened in my story leading up to this point was a blessing. God was preparing me for an opportunity that absolutely changed the direction of my life, and my family's life, forever. My experience has been a true blessing and I hope to inspire and encourage as many as will listen to what I have to teach. One of the best parts of it for me has been the ability to demonstrate in person to my four sons what hard work looks like, what taking giant risks feels like, even writing this book, and they know that it is ok to try and ok to fail. They are seeing in real time the lessons that my parents taught to me: what's the worst that can happen if you just try.

I hope that this book has helped you achieve clarity on a system that you can execute in your business in a short period of time and on a daily basis. I hope that someday, I will get to hear your stories of your success and the success of those you teach this system to on your downline or sideline, or heck, even upline! I wish you all the best, hope that you stay safe and healthy, and no matter what, JNFQ!

References

Gaille, B. (2017, May 30). *21 Direct Sales Industry Statistics and Trends*. BrandonGaille.com. https://brandongaille.com/19-direct-sales-industry-statistics-and-trends/

IBIS World. (2021, April 6). *Direct Selling Companies in the US - Market Size 2005–2027*. Www.ibisworld.com. https://www.ibisworld.com/industry-statistics/market-size/direct-selling-companies-united-states/

Accelerate Your Business Results

Visit www.directafsales.com and see some of the products Lisa Hocker has created to help you stay in consistent, purposeful, and efficient daily action!

Testimonials

I've had the pleasure to work with Lisa for years. What sets her apart from many entrepreneurs is her mental grit! She leverages that strength to push through any obstacles, find solutions and stay the course. She's tough yet transparent. She's powerful yet embraces a beginner's mind. She's a force to reckon with yet conducts herself with grace and passion. She dreams big and inspires other to dream with her. Lisa is a terrific woman, leader and friend.

Leslie Zann, Direct Selling Expert, Professional Speaker and Bestselling Author

I watched a training given by Lisa nearly two years ago, during a time when I wasn't quite sure how I'd make this business work with my corporate job and my extreme responsibilities. I logged off from her virtual training clear of three things:

1. If I wanted to be successful in this business, I could be, and it could work with my hectic life.

2. People want and need what my direct selling company has to offer, so it is necessary to keep sharing; do it early in the day before your house wakes up.

3. Nothing beats how people feel when sampling our product so get those samples into their hands and follow-up!

I've heard several of Lisa's trainings since that first one, but these lessons remain tried & true! I am inspired every time!

Dr. Tracé Dotson, Emergency Room Physician

I consider myself LUCKY to be able to benefit from the wonderful example of Lisa Hocker's leadership and training in the areas of sales, team building & her ease in handling the direct selling business in general.

I am constantly in awe of her ability to add business partners to her team, as I feel that is a huge obstacle for me. Her approach and example of leadership is very relaxed & direct. I appreciate the direct approach, no fluff…just the facts. She is extremely kind & his always willing to lend a hand to those of us (myself included) that can benefit from her experience & expertise.

Lisa is a GREAT EXAMPLE of what I would like to see for myself in this business in the future.

Heather Vanderhagen